CARNIVAL CROSSROADS

by W. G. Rogers
WHEN THIS YOU SEE REMEMBER ME: GERTRUDE STEIN IN PERSON

LIFE GOES ON

by Mildred Weston
THE SINGING HILL

CARNIVAL CROSSROADS:

the story
of Times Square

by W. G. Rogers and
Mildred Weston

DRAWINGS BY O. SOGLOW

1960
DOUBLEDAY & COMPANY, INC., GARDEN CITY, NEW YORK

9/14/60 cth R68

Library of Congress Catalog Card Number 60-9489
Copyright © 1960 by W. G. Rogers and Mildred Weston Rogers
All Rights Reserved
Printed in the United States of America
First Edition

ACKNOWLEDGMENTS

The authors are grateful for information provided by the following people professionally informed about Times Square: Sid Bernard, Captain James Leland Bozman, Captain Thomas F. Callan, Robert W. Dowling, Creighton Dunlap, Miss Grace Fields, Maurice Gralla, Herbert Hobbs, Arthur Hotaling, Jr., Ira Koenigsberg, Father Joseph A. McCaffrey, Herbert Muller, Joseph B. Shanley, Miss Helen Smith, Godfrey Stamm, and Melvin Starr; and passers-by in Times Square, clerks and store managers, the staff of the Times Square Information Center, and employees of Con Edison and various municipal departments.

In 1920 I was sent abroad to study archaeology at the American Academy in Rome. We even took field trips in those days and in a small way took part in diggings. Once you have swung a pickax that will reveal the curve of a street four thousand years covered over which was once an active, much-traveled highway, you are never quite the same again. You look at Times Square as a place about which you imagine some day scholars saying, "There appears to have been some kind of public center here."

THORNTON WILDER

WRITERS AT WORK:
The *Paris Review*
Interviews

Contents

CARNIVAL CROSSROADS

Prologue

"Where's Times Square?"

By daylight the friendly attendants at the Information Center established by New York City occasionally have that question to answer. Since it is the Times Square Information Center located in the heart of the place it's named for, they reply with a tolerant wave of the hand across the counter:

"Look around, you can't miss it."

A visitor understandably can be confused or even lost at that jumbled populous crossroads where Broadway, willfully violating the 150-year-old gridiron street pattern, slices across Seventh Avenue.

By day the famous Square takes on the slack appearance of something somebody forgot to finish: a few tall buildings to remind the stranger he has arrived in skyscraper town; more two- and three-story structures than at any other prominent spot in the metropolis; rows of false fronts as absurd as those on the saloon or dilapidated hotel in a frontier settlement; scraggly mystifying steel skeletons rearing high in the air, some with shadowy forms of letters and some apparently purposeless; and assorted crowds.

By night, however, it turns on the dazzling bright lights the world has read about and seen in the original, or viewed in photos or on the screen; and it fills up with the uncountable autos and uncountable men, women, and children. Where else on the entire earth can so many people have gathered?—millions every week, hundreds of thousands for Election Night returns, a New Year's Eve, for celebrations of all sorts, and scores of anniversaries, or to sow wild oats, shout out "Mademoiselle from Armentières," sing hymns, watch parades and parade, rejoice and sorrow.

It has not, facing on it anywhere, a single legitimate theater, though it is the hub of the theater district. It has not one TV studio, though the billing of telecasts as "direct from Times Square" or "the crossroads of the world" has lured many visitors. It has no dedicated focal point, either historical event, monument or artistic creation—no equestrian statue like the Marcus Aurelius in the Campidoglio, no towering Napoleonic column as in the Place Vendôme, no fateful ring of paving stones to mark the destruction of a Bastille, no Nelson as in Trafalgar. It has no beginning or end, no climax, design, or logic.

It is a hugely formless eruption, a growth, a kind of civic spasm, and how feverish, seething, and high strung! It is busy like an anthill, but busy aimlessly, madly, with a ceaseless scurrying for the sake of being on the go, for keeping company with others on the go, others never unwound, a perpetual-motion crowd. Except just before dawn, it never slows down or falls silent. The people gape, they exclaim, they grin at the barker making cross-eyes at the children, they hear the evangelist's fiery exhortation to come to Jesus, they sidle self-consciously past the movies promising exposés of sin and sex, they ogle the robed and turbaned giant at the Odditorium, they see Mr. Peanut wink and Little Lulu jump from the X way down to the Kleenex, and like first-grade youngsters they spell out the letters in the running news signs:

W-a-r-m   T-h-u-n-d-e-r-s-t-o-r-m-s   t-o-n-i-g-h-t

The pretty girl with her jaw sagging stares up at the Pepsi-Cola waterfall and her tall fellow smiles proudly at her and says: "Believe me now?"

The middle-aged husband and wife with the middle-aged spread pause by the window. He shakes his head and says: "Whatcha wanna lookit books for?"

The worried, cross teacher, guiding his high-school class, waves his hand and says: "Now this is west, you havta remember, west!"

A teen-age girl with a bevy of friends skips past the Paramount, clasping a photo, kissing it, rubbing it face-to across her breasts, and shrilly, almost hysterically says: "He's luscious, he's the most luscious, I love him!"

A woman points longingly at a display of furniture: "Everyone's got a chaze lounge."

A man says: "Fifteen puffs a minute."

A drab beldam in an unlighted doorway strums "Old Black Joe" on a banjo.

The city slickers have nicknames, slangy but affectionate, for out-of-towners. Hotel people dub them "the white-shoe trade" in summer. At all seasons the sight-seeing bus driver or barker refers to "hicksters"; the lunchroom manager, to "farmers"; and the theater crowd, to "popeyes."

"They're the best people in the world," a restaurant proprietor declared emphatically. "They are the most affable, the least demanding, the most patient" of all customers in the opinion of the owner of a chain of candy stores. "They're very fine folks," according to the bus-tour promoter, his hair plastered back, a stickpin in his tie, a glib talker who, with his hands in his pockets, paced the creaking floor of his bare office. "They know a lot more about New York than a lot of New Yorkers, too." He asked: "How many New Yorkers ever wen' up the Empire State, or the Statue o' Libetty?" He added: "I never did myself."

Maybe some natives wouldn't know where Times Square is, either, that is, exactly what street begins it, and where it ends.

A century and a half ago a foreigner regarded Lower Broadway as "already the city's chief sight," and it still may claim that rating for the stretch between 42nd Street and 47th, the core of Times Square, thanks mainly to the dancing lights and indefatigable crowds. Actress Peggy Wood described Times Square as "the actor's campus . . . our training ground and our school . . . the heart of our city, our theater, and therefore our culture." Guidebook editors, authors, and other observers have saluted it with exuberant superlatives:

"The brightest night spot on earth."

"A scintillation which has no equal in America or anywhere else in the world."

"The focal point of America's good time—the No. 1 tourist attraction in the Nation's No. 1 tourist town . . . the world's flashiest invitation to fun."

"The entertainment capital and showcase of the country."

"The accepted symbol of gaiety, glitter and good wild oats. To leave New York without having seen Times Square is unthinkable; thanks to its location, it is also almost impossible."

It is, of course, a mammoth salesroom, a Square chockful of bait. It surpasses its competitors in being more guileful and ruthless. "Hi sucker!" it greets everyone, and after one nibble you're hooked. Right on the Square proper you can buy books, clothes for men and women, cigars, cigarettes, drugs, furniture, picture postcards and comic postcards, records, toys, tricks, religious statuettes and medals, colored prints of Jesus and Mary, colored photos of nudes, rubber dummies of men making water, cameras, airplane reservations, foreign currency. You can bank there, eat and sleep, hear a sermon, find a girl to dance with, drink with or what have you, and right around the corner attend a wedding or a funeral.

Hawk-eyed bus-tour agents mounting watch at the intersections, flaunting printed signs tucked in the bands of their visored caps to advertise their business, claim they can spot the hickster nine times out of ten. He, or she, wears vacation clothes, or a suit wrinkled from a night in a coach. He star-gazes. He carries a leather-cased camera on a shoulder strap, and a guidebook and a map. He walks slowly. He has a rosy-cheeked, corn-fed look. He has a convention badge and ribbon pinned to his lapel. He holds hands with his bride, who sports an orchid, probably wilted.

If they overhear him say, "Excuse me, please," it's a dead give-away.

Both natives and out-of-towners proliferate here. A count of 800 taken at different hours of an August week shows they run approximately half and half, just folks from Manhattan, Brooklyn, and all the boroughs, and just folks from Alabama, California, Indiana, Kentucky, Maryland, Massachusetts, Michigan, Mississippi, Missouri, New Hampshire, New Jersey, New York, North Carolina, Ohio, Oregon, Pennsylvania, South Carolina and Texas, and from Australia, Brazil, Canada, Cuba, England, Finland, France, Germany, Holland, Mexico, Puerto Rico, Salvador, Saudi Arabia, Turkey, and Trinidad.

And that isn't all. Hotalings Out-of-Town Newspapers, at the northern end of the Times Tower, stocks 330 different United States papers, and daily purchases represent 250 to 300 cities.

Whether New York is their habitat or they hail from the ends of the earth, these people work at many professions, jobs, and callings. The same poll lists accountant, actor, advertising man, air hostess, baker, banker, butler, clerk, chemist, contractor, dancer, driver, florist, hobo, housewife, jeweler, laborer, lawyer, mechanic, minister, musician, nurse, physician, policeman, prize fighter, secretary, social worker, soda jerk, student, tailor, telephone operator, writer.

What are they doing here? What do they expect? They have Broadways and midways of their own, and local movies as new as those in first-run houses; they have their own amusement parks, dance halls, restaurants, especially their TV programs. They don't come to feed the pigeons as in St. Mark's, to cheer a harangue as in the Piazza Venezia, to revere a tomb as in the Red Square, to sit at the Café de la Paix as in the Place de l'Opéra.

Many of them, of course, go through the Square because it's on the shortest line between two points. They come from Larchmont, Rye, Garden City, Irvington, Orange, they are the transients on the way to or from the theater, home, Grand Central, Penn Station, or bus terminal. They swing a brief case, they buy a paper, they glance at the news flashes, but always they whisk into sight and out again in a mad hurry, more conscious of time than of Times Square. Or it's evening, they are with their wives, they stop for peanut candy, or ice cream, or a drink, it was a good show, it's another day.

They get the full feel and sense, if not the feel and non-sense, of that dizzy whirligig spot only after a stay of some length. In winter they see the mists blown across the lights to veil them intermittently, the snow settled on Father Duffy's bronze shoulders, the steam whistling out of the black manholes, the slush lying deep at the curbs, the ragged and unkempt vendor of roasted chestnuts. In spring young girls blossom forth in colored dresses and pretty hats, unsophisticated, un-big-city-like, incongruous in these worldly surroundings. Summer and fall bring the throngs of loungers, the sport shirt, the sandals and the dark glasses at the fruit-drink stands, the blind man with the tap-tap-tapping cane, the blind woman with a jangling cup, the evangelists and pamphleteers, the gangs of kids in skin-tight jeans with shiny buttons, the laborer in the excavation entertained by his own radio 10 feet below the pavement, the unshaven face, the besotted face, the clean honest face, the one too pallid and narrow between the eyes, the fellow with a swept-wing hair-do, slightly touched brows, molded and polished hair and earrings, a kind of sweater boy.

But even for a weekend, an evening, an hour, they come, they come from a block away, or a mile, or a thousand miles, they pour in by the millions. The equivalent of twice, or perhaps three times, the population of the entire United States sweeps through like a tide every year.

They come because they are lonely. Because they didn't like where they were. Because they have troubles and don't know what to do except forget them in the heart of a multitude. Because they want fun. Because they are on a binge. Because they must have a man, a woman, a card game, dice, drink, or dope. Because it's the most publicized place in the world. Because it's the section everybody back home talks about. Because Times Square is the big deal, because this is the life. Because they'll be seen, because they won't be seen. Because they find the Playlands, the movies, the shooting galleries, the cup of coffee, the souvenir, the pin-ball tables, and that temptation saluted and sung so zest-fully in *Guys and Dolls:* "The oldest established permanent floating crap game in New York."

Perhaps most often it is the herd instinct. The crowd drawn by the lights comes also to view the rest of the crowd drawn by the lights. It pyramids. "Most of the time the really interesting sight to the Roman crowd in the forum was the crowd itself, exactly as in Times Square," Simeon Strunsky wrote. "The omnipresent interest of New York—to New Yorkers themselves as well as outsiders—is the pass-ing throng, the great flux, the moving mass of people on the streets," according to John C. Van Dyke.

"You want to know what kind of clerks we like to have in Times Square?" asked the candy-store woman. "The most outgoing kind there is. People come in there, they want to talk, and they want to be talked to."

As for sweets, she added: "They want what they don't get at home."

That holds true for a lot of other things.

They get there by traveling in any direction, for all roads lead to Times Square. Footpath, dirt lane, crowned black asphalt, and broad white-striped highway with miles of flashing green lights and "go" signals speed the immeas-urable crowds with a clangor, thunder, and carbon mon-oxide stench on to "the Crossroads of the World."

Geographically it lies out on the country's extreme edge. But swarms of people of all languages, colors and races, rich and poor, lame and strong, honest and not, the man in sweater, in Levis or fez or silk hat, the woman in obi, sari, sack, slacks or jewels, the countless millions attracted to it hypnotically day and night, haul it back by sheer weight into the demographic American middle.

A single route leads straight there all the distance down from Albany, or maybe the North Pole; and along the last lap, buses, trucks, tourist autos, business cars, models with fins and jalopies, find it handily one-way southbound, too. You shove afoot through loud-mouthed, jostling bands that stalk the sidewalks on 42nd Street. You are funneled along a darker side street, banal, dingy vestibule to the magnificent electric brilliance of the Square itself. You enter from down under by subway.

You advance through smells—sweat, perfume, tobacco, sodden breath of whiskey and beer, pizza-pie tang, whiff of coffee, sickly sweet of burnt sugar, fetid odors seeping up from underground through bars and gratings. You advance through noises—angry horns, tires, motors, doorman's and policeman's whistle, foreign and native tongues, panhandler's spiel and evangelist's preaching, barker's pitch, shuffle of feet, radio blare, or most unexpectedly, a breeze soughing in trees or a steady pounding waterfall.

All this is Times Square today. How did it get this way? For that answer, you may come in the back door, from the past, and see for yourself. Architects and builders stake out the uptown progress with store, hotel, and apartment. Advertisers guide you from oil lamp to gas mantle to incandescent bulb to neon tubing and so to the spectacular displays unrivaled anywhere in the world. You follow the press, or even Adolph S. Ochs alone, up from Park Row via Greeley and Herald Squares. You track the nighttime path of the theaters from way downtown to Union Square and 34th Street, trampling over the cabbage patches, paving the fields and footways with knobby cobbles, reaching right up Broadway for the crucial bold leap into Times Square. You're on the trail of burlesque, Minsky's and everybody else's. The elegant restaurant and lobster palaces pass in review; there is a sinister line-up of thieves, gangsters, and murderers.

1 "Innumerable people passed from one shore and the other in order to see us"

It was four and a half centuries ago in April—always the start of the sight-seeing season—that a European first set out in the direction of our Times Square. He never would have believed how many billions followed him.

At the tip of Manhattan, water lapped the rocks and the sedges gently. Green covered everything. The beautiful pale springtime color showed in every direction, along the flat shore beyond which the sun set, ahead on the low-lying islands or to the rear in the nondescript waste of scrub, field, marsh, and woods, or as we say, Battery Park, Broadway and the bustling streets which after years and years reached Times Square.

Through the Narrows in the near distance, within the arm of the future Coney Island in the future Gravesend Bay, a caravel lay at anchor. Arched as steeply as a gravy boat, it had bobbed and skittered up the coast from the Carolinas-to-be. Though Columbus could have mistaken it with its three masts square-rigged and lateen-rigged for one of his own fleet, it was the *Dauphine*. It flew both the French flag with the sheaflike fleur-de-lis on a blue base and, just under it, the navy's blue and red pennant.

Built in Le Havre, the port Francis I founded as Havre de Grâce, and named for his son new born at Amboise, the 100-tonner belonged with a foursome of ships assigned by the monarch to the ocean crossing. Storms sank two of them, and put the third out of commission. Left alone for the perilous adventure, heavy with provisions for eight months, the *Dauphine* had reduced by a half its normal crew of one hundred. All Normans, they had sailed from Dieppe, with Captain Antoine de Conflans in command. However they rated with him, they were heartily despised by a crusty foreigner aboard, a subordinate, too, mere pilot and navigator, but the representative of an experienced and superior race of seamen, the most important single personage on the *Dauphine* and perhaps even in sixteenth-century American history:

Giovanni da Verrazano, or as his French masters spelt it, Jehan de Verrasanne. History salutes him as discoverer of the mouth of the Hudson and New York harbor in 1524.

Born about 1485 in Val di Greve, a few miles south of Florence, he already felt more at home on the bounding Atlantic than most of his contemporaries when, nearly forty years old, he persuaded Francis I to let him probe along the middle of North America for the mythical passage to Cathay. His head bushy, his brow imperiously furrowed, his armored chest bulging like a barrel as Ettore Ximenes sculptured him four centuries later for a statue in Battery Park, he possessed the presence, the romantic appeal or the wit to inveigle the usually shrewd merchants of Lyons into financing his dubious mission.

Willfully expecting nothing of this tremendous continent except a passage through it, he fooled himself into thinking that a sea washed right across North America almost to

the Pacific. Not content to find what did not exist, he also failed to find what in glorious prospect did: the developing Upper Bay, the high-speed streets and avenues that would expand out of crude trails, and the shores where solid green would vanish under a solid sheath of the brick, steel, and glass, often colorless, of warehouse, office, dock, apartment, and factory.

It was none of the function of the captain to put down his sword for the pen and leave a written record. The clerical task fell to Verrazano. He noted the Hudson, and paid respectful homage to the French king's ancient title by christening this New World domain Angoulême. We are happy to learn that he liked what he saw:

"A very agreeable situation located within two small prominent hills, in the midst of which flowed to the sea a very great river, which was deep within the mouth, and from the sea to the hills of that place with the rising of the tides, which we found eight feet, any laden ship might have passed."

If this is a quotation from Verrazano, then, in the words of Count Giulio Maccho de Cellere of Rome, it constituted "the birth certificate of New York." On the dutiful explorer's return to Dieppe he dispatched an official letter to Francis. It has been lost. But he also informed several Florentine friends, who took better care of their mail. This communication to one of them about the wide navigable river was unearthed in the Cellere collection, and quashed whatever doubts still persisted about Verrazano's pioneering exploit.

What happened to this harbinger of the modern metropolis? According to one opinion, Charles V of Spain captured him and was happy to hang him for piracy. According to another, he made some natives of the West Indies even happier: the savages seized him and several companions, tortured them, chopped them up, roasted and ate them. But he succeeded in entering the bay, and reconnoitering in a small boat, although the threat of a storm suddenly scared him off and he never returned. Though he missed Times Square itself, and never set foot on the Promised Land, this adventurer, this Moses, was blessed with an infallible sense of direction, and of destiny.

More than a discoverer, he was a prophet. He recognized in the inquisitive natives who came paddling about him and his sailors the direct ancestors of the present-day population of Times Square. The first recorded comment, and it is Verrazano's, about these men and women already on the spot classified them specifically as sight-seers. His letter in the Cellere codex described the Indians swarming over the bay and running down to the water's edge. They rode about in 30 barges or canoes, and in his words:

"Innumerable people passed from one shore and the other in order to see us."

Times Square's jammed sidewalks and pavement, noise and lights, barker and goggle-eyed tourist originated then and there in the nosy redskin braves and squaws and the seafarers. Everybody came out to stare.

II "Disgraceful and dastardly"

It was a short jump north to midtown but it took centuries. Starting from tiny Bowling Green where, as everybody says though nobody ever proves, Peter Minuit struck his famous $24 bargain with the Indians, New Yorkers in their deliberate progress ticked off such milestones as the Canal, the Wall and the Collect Pond called Kolch by the Dutch. Marsh land dipped away on one side and gray ledges of rock reared up on the other. For its entire length or sections of it, the principal meandering route bore through the years enough different names to confuse a traveler, instead of aiding him, and they too constituted a kind of milestone: Great Wagon Way, the unromantic Dutch identified it; Great George Street, according to the English still loyal to the king; and formally or in fun, the Middle Road, the Boulevard, the Rialto, Ladies' Mile, Jarvis's Parade, and Bloomingdale Road before it ultimately styled itself Broadway simple, plain, and world-renowned.

The first Americans to stage an entrance in Times Square momentously and with appropriate fanfare were General George Washington and General Israel Putnam.

In 1776 Putnam carried on where the European explorers left off; the torch they dropped at the bottom of Manhattan he picked up at No. 1 Broadway, establishing headquarters there for the Battle of Long Island. "Old Wolf," as they dubbed him, had fought at Bunker Hill, and transferred with Washington to New York when Howe's fleet and army threatened it. He found a different city, as wanton as Boston had been puritanical. Every night the provost dungeon filled up with roistering soldiers and their women tumbled in there in amorous couples to be sorted out only in the morning. It sapped the discipline of an army due at war at any minute.

The commander in chief, slimmer and taller than Putnam, and forty-four years old to his fifty-eight, had also occupied a downtown Broadway address until Martha joined him and they settled in more elegant and spacious Richmond Hill, at Varick and Charlton Streets, where Aaron Burr would live and, briefly, President John Quincy Adams. The very day before the enemy attack, Washington had moved again to the northern end of his line, to the Roger Morris house, or the Jumel Mansion, at 161st Street, overlooking his Harlem village along 125th Street as well as our Polo Grounds.

At eleven in the morning of a hot, bright, and clear Sunday, September 15, five of Howe's frigates drew up in the East River just off Kip's Bay, and opened fire point-blank on the brigade posted there with its back to Murray Hill and its right stretching toward the Parade Ground. Those massed batteries, which both American commanders awaited with dread and against which neither could offer any defense, set the two men off at breakneck speed to cover the ten miles separating them. To leave again on the spur of the moment confirmed the popular Putnam legend.

41755

When the news of Lexington reached him on his Connecticut farm, he had abandoned his plow in its furrow and galloped to the scene of the crisis in Massachusetts. Now again he dashed posthaste for the rendezvous which has furnished Times Square with its most cogent claim to historical status.

In little more than an hour, General Sir Henry Clinton's assault force of 4000 brushed back the flabby Continentals, overran Robert Murray's place, Inklenberg, and spread out along the Post Road. Now Mrs. Murray got her chance, according to a second story that everybody tells and nobody proves, to entertain Howe and mesmerize him into dallying long enough for the Americans to flee. Howe was deliberate anyway, and luck instead of a wily hostess extricated the demoralized soldiers.

With Putnam racing on ahead, young Aaron Burr, familiar with the terrain since boyhood, guided the general's ragged forces to the junction of Broadway and 43rd Street, in our terminology. A plaque on the old Putnam Building, predecessor of the Paramount Building, marked this rallying point. But with a 43rd Street lacking, Lon's Lane, or Steuben Street, as it was named at one end and the other, wandered cater-cornered from that intersection southerly past our Bryant Park to the East River at the upper edge of Kip's Bay, around 37th Street. The unpretentious path led between stone walls which guarded the cultivated fields stretching out beyond them on each side, and might also serve as breastworks for defending troops.

Washington saw his men turn tail at Clinton's onslaught, yet with that brigade routed, he could still rely on two more, thanks to Putnam's march uptown. General John Fellows had swung his column first into the narrow lane, and moved in far enough to leave room behind him for General Samuel H. Parsons'. The commander in chief ordered a stand. But the unfaltering advance of the Britishers, a small body but trim, fully equipped, in scarlet uniforms, threw a fright into the uneven, unmilitary array of raw Continentals, and they refused to obey.

Where movie, auction room, bar, shoe store, ticket agency, one-arm restaurant, drugstore, candy counter or Playland grub today for a fast buck, where streets thunder with traffic louder than the ping of a whole arsenal of muskets, and where the terrain is mined with subways, the panicky Americans fled over open fields. A pitiful sight in their civilian clothes and buckle shoes, sweaty and disheveled, they dragged their unwieldy flintlocks behind them, unless they threw them away, and the useless powder horn and shot pouch slapped at their hips as they ran.

For all his gold epaulettes, his blue and buff, his stylish three-cornered hat and his swallowtails buttoned back for the saddle, and for all his rank and prestige, too, Washington lost control over them, and over himself. In a rage he rode them down. He lashed them over the shoulders with his crop. He cursed them. They were too scared to make a stand. No one had drilled courage into them yet. Overwhelmed with despair at the "disgraceful and dastardly" rout, he numbly sat his horse in Bryant Park and watched in a daze as the enemy drew within one hundred yards, and then eighty. He seemed resigned to capture. An alert soldier seized the bridle of his mount and hurried him to safety.

An unexpected success the next day provided American morale with a tragically needed boost: Colonel Thomas Knowlton stood immovable against the frontal attacks of bare-kneed, busbied Scotch Highlanders on the slopes west of the site of Columbia University. Washington clung to strong positions in the northern end of the island till Howe outflanked him, and then retreated through New Jersey and into Pennsylvania. He would wait only to year's end to even the score, and more, by crossing the Delaware to catch Trenton by surprise on Christmas Night 1776.

When at long last the fighting ended and the new young government was formed, New York as the temporal capital drew Washington back for the beginning months of his Presidency. A favorite drive in the family coach with the first First Lady was the "14 miles around." The dignified and handsome Washington, now in civilian clothes, and his wife in simple homespun and a plain cap, began their ride in Franklin Square and Cherry Street, next headed up the Post Road, and turned over Apthorp Lane and then down the Bloomingdale Road. They crossed our 42nd Street on Broadway. That carried Washington near the stone walls where Putnam's men had broken, and could have reminded him of the calamitous September hour when the Revolutionary cause must have seemed doomed

In this sparsely settled, rolling countryside, there was hardly a house in sight. Washington remembered these fields swarming with soldiers, perhaps 10,000 of them. Would anyone else ever see such a mighty concourse in this isolated place? It didn't seem possible.

III "To their astonishment, found themselves rich men"

In the month of August before Howe and Clinton drove Washington from New York, he had requisitioned as a hospital for his troops a place named Frog Hall. The property of Joseph Haynes, a British sympathizer, it was situated about in the middle of our 44th Street just west of Broadway. Wolfert Webber built it.

That takes us in one jump from George Washington to Washington Irving, and to two intriguing possibilities: that Irving wrote the first Times Square love story, and that Times Square was once a cabbage patch—as the noble Roman forum was once a lowly pasture.

Cobus Webber, unless it was Arnoult—that was long dim years ago—came over first from Holland in the early eighteenth century. By 1713 he owned Great Kill Farm at the mouth of the creek, or kill, on the Hudson near our 34th Street. When this wide acreage fell into the possession of Hoppes, or Hoppers, and of the Nortons who lived in the Hermitage west on 42nd Street, the Webbers moved north to Great Kill hamlet, the exact region where Times Square would develop. By a present-day map, Wolfert Webber's expansive holdings reached from Sixth Avenue across

Bloomingdale Road, or Broadway, and on westward, and from 41st Street to 49th. It was around those green meadows that his fellow Dutchmen settled. The industrious burghers occupied sprawling houses; buttonwood trees shaded their lawns, which had borders of white picket fences. Flocks of swallows and martins filled the air. Rows on rows of turnips and cabbages, the democratic vegetables, surrounded these tidy New World homesteads.

If Irving's *Wolfert Webber,* or *Golden Dreams* celebrates this crossroads, then it surpasses everything else written about the intersection either as good dirt farm or as steel-and-asphalt fabrication.

Authors have not ignored Times Square. They devote a sentence, a paragraph or a chapter to it; they even paid homage in one entire novel and one novella. Their characters fix up dates at the Out-of-Town Newspaper racks, patronize the popular hotels and restaurants, or enjoy the theater. Walt Whitman often visited the Crystal Palace at the World's Fair only a block to the east. Theodore Dreiser saluted this center exuberantly: "Here is the great city, and it is lush and dreamy." But Irving led the way with the quaint mixture of fact and fiction put into the mouth of his Diedrich Knickerbocker:

The first Webber, though he arrived when the dynamic Oloffe Van Kortlandt bossed the thriving colony, nourished no more exalted an ambition than to raise cabbages. Several generations later his descendant Wolfert was pinched for money for his daughter's dowry because progress was conspiring against him. The restless city had branched out inexorably around the frustrated farmer, squeezing him in, robbing him of the chance to prosper after the family fashion. Neighbors' pigs rooted in his gar-

den, and their urchins climbed his fences and trespassed in his yard. He was "hemmed in by streets and houses, which intercepted air and sunshine"—so many years ago, before people ever imagined skyscrapers, did they complain of the handicaps of Gotham!

Dirk Waldron sued for the hand of his pretty teen-aged Amy. The distraught father did not approve. While his expenses doubled or tripled, his cabbages stayed the same size. He earned so little he could not afford to surrender an inch of ground as dowry, even for the sake of a boy he liked. In despair he caught at one last hope. Other islanders were hunting for treasure reported buried by Peter Stuyvesant. Wolfert dug, too, in his own garden where, without uncovering a single coin, he damaged his crop and hastened his ruin.

Discouraged and defeated, he felt life ebb away, whereupon his lawyer hurried to congratulate the daughter astonished to find herself an heiress: fields of no value for growing cabbages brought fabulous prices from the growing city. Amy and Dirk, collecting a handsome inheritance, could live happily ever afterward.

Irving drew a moral: "Wolfert Webber was one of those worthy Dutch burghers of the Manahattoes whose fortunes have been made, in a manner, in spite of themselves; who have tenaciously held on to their hereditary acres, raising turnips and cabbages about the streets of the city, hardly able to make both ends meet, until the corporation has cruelly driven streets through their abodes, and they have suddenly awakened out of their lethargy, and, to their astonishment, found themselves rich men."

Irving concluded: "Before many months had elapsed, a great bustling street passed through the very centre of the

Webber garden, just where Wolfert had dreamed of finding a treasure."

Irving knew every foot of this setting, of course. In 1803, John Jacob Astor foreclosed on land owned by both Webber and Medcef Eden—the Astor Hotel stands on the site of the Eden farmhouse. Irving was Astor's friend, indeed perhaps too subservient a friend, even a factotum. His "great bustling street" sounds like Broadway, even Broadway at Seventh Avenue just where Astor started to accumulate a fortune in real estate. For that matter, the example of Astor may have inspired the portrait of the Webbers and Waldrons who prospered by sitting tight.

IV "An ambitious little row of houses"

New York didn't invade the future Times Square frontally, but by flanking routes. It thrust columns to the east and west to encircle its prey before finally drawing in from all sides pincers-fashion. The city acted shy toward the crossroads. It couldn't quite decide how to handle so much open roadway and such misshapen parcels of land. Should it be proud or ashamed? The giant lopsided X formed by Broadway and Seventh Avenue, an X more than half a mile around, and chopped into layers by the six streets from 42nd to 47th, didn't look so much like a civic opportunity as just sort of a mess.

Because of this, New York in the abstract, New York anonymous, overran the place. The explorers, generals, farmers, cabbage growers, lasses and their lovers vanished in the crowd. It was only at the end of the nineteenth century, when traffic began to converge there, that the simple dirt crossroads perked up with a hint of developing into the crossroads of the world. Until then, the historic personages and currents, the priests, officials, entrepreneurs, and realtors, bypassed the old Dutch truck gardens. They traveled north via Fifth and Eighth Avenues. Broadway in our midtown was all bumps, ruts, and potholes. Squatters in hovels scrounged a living out beyond Times Square, and bony dogs in harness dragged the carts in which they scavenged. On that deserted and lonely route a bus could overturn on a winter night and kill the unwary driver. Nobody went there who mattered until the day when suddenly everybody who mattered went.

When Irving wrote about the Webbers, the city's population had reached 100,000. In 1811, or around the same time, John Randall, Jr., laid out the gridiron pattern, cutting up the entire island like a pan of fudge into streets and avenues; a mathematical, dull, and uninventive job, he could have done it with a lead pencil and an ordinary ruler, with never a thought for the fateful graphite smudge at Broadway, Seventh, and 42nd. The self-conscious commissioners who assigned the task to Randall commented, somewhat abashedly, that folks might "laugh" at the provision for "a greater population than is collected at any one spot this side of China." They couldn't laugh long. In 1850 the count climbed to half a million men, women, and children, and nearer a million by the outbreak of the Civil War. Mayor Fernando Wood, with a covetous eye on Brooklyn and other expanding neighborhoods, could forecast "one compact city."

New York grew not block by block but by leaps and bounds. It thrust forth a chain of villages as a plant sends out runners: Chelsea, Great Kill, Harsenville, Bloomingdale, Manhattanville, Harlem; and then filled in the spots left vacant. In the 1840s diarist George Templeton Strong observed that at last some one was putting up along 42nd Street "an ambitious little row of houses"—houses for Everyman. Epidemics of yellow fever or cholera, the longing for

shade, lawn and breezes, and the overwhelming pressure of immigrants all squeezed people, unknown people, clerks, laborers, carpenters, draymen, hostlers, printers, tradesmen, well-to-do and ne'er-do-well out of the crowded southernmost corner and inched their community farther and farther north, valley to town to city to metropolis to Gotham. Land speculators smarter than Webbers reaped fortunes by betting on expansion, which averaged about a mile every twenty years.

The 22nd Ward, including Times Square, was carved out of the old 19th in 1853. Four separate buildings occupied the triangle where the Times Tower stands, and two more rose to modest heights across Seventh Avenue, to the west. Vacant lots lined the east side of Broadway from 42nd to 44th. But by 1879, and perhaps earlier, structures of two to four stories took up the entire Times Square frontage, and three buildings instead of four appeared on the site of the newspaper. Like good suburbanites the anonymous residents picked flowers, tended lawns, gazed at the moon and stars and no doubt bird-watched, too, where today no creatures at all fly except pigeons, sparrows, and the red-winged Budweiser eagle, and nothing grows except fourteen London plane trees and enough hedge for a wheelbarrow load.

For a while Fifth Avenue held the lead in its uptown race with Broadway. It had won an easy lap, for instance, on July 4, 1842, when it staged a parade to inaugurate the Croton Reservoir between 40th and 42nd Streets. Right across Fifth, the holiday public could sit down to plates of ice cream in a little yellow house in a wide yard where cows had grazed and chickens scratched, but the immense reservoir itself had a massive cosmopolitan look. Sloping walls soared fifty feet from a base half again as thick. The main eastern entrance wreathed in ivy admitted citizens to the promenade along the top, where a placid four-acre lake storing 24,000,000 gallons of water reflected the sky and clouds, and where a vista of miles of roofs stretched off to the south, and partly developed country to the north.

But the restive population, which could have wondered what Fifth Avenue had that Sixth did not, or Broadway, either, shifted substantially westward in 1853. Envious of the crowds attracted to the World's Fair in Hyde Park, London, New Yorkers decided to build their own. A block nearer the site of Times Square, it would afford a kind of preview of the bustling Square itself.

An impresario got a permit to erect a Crystal Palace, American-style, though modeled closely on Sir Joseph Paxton's, in Madison Square at an estimated cost of $150,000. But Madison Square protested emphatically against the use of its greensward for profit even with an avowedly artistic purpose. If it let the bars down once, wouldn't Niblo and Barnum, too, arguing that they were cultural, move in with an amusement garden, circus, or museum? The sponsors yielded, and as a substitute proposed Reservoir Square, our Bryant Park, between the Reservoir and Sixth Avenue, "as being next in importance, with respect to location and size."

Architects Georg J. B. Carstensen and Charles Gildemeister wrote a pamphlet about the construction. The first column was raised with ceremonies October 30, 1852. The pair took pains to deny all blame for the sometimes halting progress. Among many hindrances they cited their lack of control over contracts; consequently they couldn't prevent delays due, for instance, to a senseless delivery schedule by which they got the beams for a balcony before the beams for the basement on which the balcony rested. Just over 1300 feet long, the native Crystal Palace still was little more than a third as big as the one re-erected in Sydenham, England. Its legislative charter identified the organizers as the Association for the Exhibition of the Industry of All Nations.

While the reservoir beside it resembled some ancient pyramidal structure destined for the banks of the Nile, the Palace didn't look as though it belonged with any river yet discovered, not the Nile, Thames, or Hudson. It was a flat, square-sided cake with gobs of fancy frosting. Even more incongruous, there sprang up directly across 42nd Street the skeletal and peaked Latting Observatory, a junior Eiffel Tower of iron and wood built by Warren Latting.

The Crystal Palace advertised worth-while sights, among them all-American items like sewing machines, new plows, and an elevator which functioned; a second one ran in the Observatory. Europe lent Bertel Thorwaldsen's marble Apostles, and paintings, fine woods, fabrics and the handicraft of renowned silversmiths, according to a constant, and articulate visitor, Walt Whitman.

But many exhibitions offered gaudy, Coney Island attractions. Art drew the social upper crust, never yet big enough to make a World's Fair pay. So as a come-on for the masses, the publicity-wise management also displayed an alligator, anaconda, dancing bear and six-legged calf, a fat woman, Lilliputians and giants, and deafening steam calliopes. It wasn't yet Times Square but it was the flashy Times Square idea, indiscriminate, frenzied, and maybe a bit foreboding, midway, playland, and side show rolled into one.

From the halfway level of the Observatory, as well as the summit, sight-seers enjoyed breath-taking views of traffic lumbering along Broadway a block and a half to the west. Heavy market wagons with a clatter of iron-rimmed wheels drove downtown in the morning, and at all hours vehicles of all shapes and sizes rolled past. The Observatory burned in 1856, and the Palace in 1858. But while the queer structures lasted, they had a prophetic present-day air and sight and sound around them. Pennants flew from the towers and domes of the glass-walled temple where the public swarmed like pilgrims. People arrived in colorful family groups or one by one, men on horseback, the rich in carriages, the middle class in omnibuses, the poor afoot. Ladies in hoop skirts draped shawls over their shoulders; men with stovepipe hats strutted about in tight-fitting trousers; the boys hung around in suits as stiff as their fathers'. The heathen Chinee sported pigtails. The same crowd, though in different dress, a thousand times as large and a thousand times as eager to see and be seen, packs Times Square today.

V "The abode
of the gods"

The first man ever to conjure up in Times Square a typical seething, shoving, theater-mad crowd was a cigar maker. At that period, forty years after the Crystal Palace, it wasn't yet Times Square, but Longacre Square. The cigar maker was also inventor, composer, impresario, and general entrepreneur, a German immigrant, an orthodox Jew, a scrapper with a jumpy temper, a practical joker, and a genius at showmanship.

He was Oscar Hammerstein I, usually regarded as "the father of Times Square," a title he must deserve since no one else claims it, unless of course anyone else would prefer to repudiate the place nowadays. By a coincidence, the only sound at which this noisy intersection cringes, the hiss, became the sound to which it partly owes its existence. Hammerstein, jumping to his feet in his box at the theater, did the hissing.

Underlying his theatrical career was his success as inventor. One of his contraptions molded twelve cigars in a single operation. Another consisted of a suction system for spreading and shaping tobacco leaves. He patented a rolling machine, a heading machine, and a cutter; a leg-baker which applied heat directly to an injury, and an inkwell which closed automatically. From his frenetic career as impresario he stole many hours to tinker with the one hundred or so gadgets he devised. He reserved rooms in two of his Times Square properties for a workbench, and in the same quarters installed a piano at which he composed the musical numbers he could persuade himself as producer to produce in a theater he could persuade himself as owner to lease.

New York City formally invaded Longacre Square with the opening in 1895 of Hammerstein's Olympia; as an entertainment catch-all, it continued the carnival tradition of the Crystal Palace.

Born in 1847, Hammerstein had turned only thirty-three when in 1880 he built the Harlem Opera House, first theater north of Central Park. Compared to this seven-league leap, Times Square would require only one safe short step. He put up the Manhattan Opera House on 34th Street between Broadway and Seventh Avenue in 1892, and then a second one in 1906 two blocks farther west. Here the jealous Metropolitan Opera bought him out, lowering the curtain on a healthy artistic rivalry, and extorted from him a promise, on which he would renege hot-headedly, to stay out of the field. Here also to win a niche in our music hall of fame, he gave the American premières of *Louise*, *Pelléas et Mélisande* and *Elektra*. In 1891 at the Lenox Lyceum at 59th Street and Madison Avenue, he presented the first formal *Cavalleria Rusticana* in New York. Though Mascagni's one-acter would grow into a perennial favorite, the box office that night proved so disastrous that Hammerstein salvaged nothing except the wry satisfaction of a pun: he threatened to change the title to *Cavalleria Busticana*.

54

Hardly five feet and a half tall, portly, with a goatee, always smoking a long black cigar, he wore a Prince Albert coat with velvet lapels and striped pants black and white, gray, or fawn-colored. On his Tuesday afternoon "at home" tryouts, the more ludicrous amateur acts could reduce him to helpless laughter so that he sneaked away and left an assistant to break the news to the hapless aspirant. He rebuffed a girl from Colorado ambitious to appear at his Victoria Theater: she did not qualify, and he hired only celebrities. But he could teach her how to become one: dress in a cowboy's togs, ride a horse through Broadway to his Times Square theater, and sing there till a cop arrested her. She got the job.

Working out one of his own compositions, with his inevitable silk hat on the back of his head as he thumped the keyboard, he would light on the note or phrase that suited him, toss the hat in the air in jubilation, tumble over a chair to catch it, and hustle off to some other task. An invitingly picturesque subject for feature writers, he granted an interview to one from the *Times*. The reporter described an impresario so absent-minded, if not so intent on graver matters, that he slammed a two-pound paperweight onto his own hat on his desk, and later pulled a paper box down over his ears as headgear. To the newsman bidding him good-by, Hammerstein urged, "Have a cigar," and pressed on him a thick cork penholder in the shape of a cigar.

"The Old Man," as associates knew him, forbade the cry "bravo" in his houses. To watch his productions he sat backstage on a kitchen chair. He passed out quarters to newsboys. It also tickled the rogue to slip these coins down the back of opera diva Emma Trentini.

He deliberately cooked up a quarrel with Yvette Guilbert

55

to oust her from his theater where she earned him big money so he could present his own *Marguerite* based on *Faust*. *Munsey's* magazine praised it as "a deft combination of living pictures, ballet, fence posters and circus act," but that hardly suggested the equal of the French *chanteuse*. The *Times*, though rating scenery and costumes magnificent, disparaged Hammerstein's score with the devastating comment that it would do.

He swapped blows with a livery-stable employee, and an alderman.

In his Manhattan Opera House No. 1, he hissed Marietta de Dio, a singer, and precipitated a rough-and-tumble with the girl's devoted sponsor. With its 2600 seats and fifty boxes, this place by the fall of 1894 belonged jointly to Hammerstein and the music-hall pair Koster and Bial. They sold food and drink, he billed the acts. George Kessler, salesman for Moët et Chandon, in addition to his legitimate interest in the French champagne, took an extracurricular interest in the French girl. When he tried to persuade Hammerstein to book her American debut in the Manhattan, Hammerstein refused. Rashly going over his head, Kessler appealed to Koster and Bial, who agreed.

The elated Kessler occupied a box on Marietta's first night. In one right beside him sat Hammerstein itching to get even. When the audience applauded the newcomer, Hammerstein stood up so that everybody could identify him, and hissed. Kessler remonstrated. Hammerstein upbraided him furiously.

Stamping out angrily to the promenade, the men put on a more exciting show than what the public paid to see on the other side of the footlights. The very names Kessler, Koster, Bial, Marietta, and Oscar read like the cast of an

old-time melodrama. Hammerstein demanded Kessler's arrest, but the policeman on duty, figuring he himself could get hurt the most in this scrap, walked cagily out of sight and hearing. Hammerstein at once sailed into his enemy again. No doubt they staged an amateurish bout with plenty of huffing and puffing, wild swings and misses by a mile, but they did fight. Ushers bounced them into the street, where they flailed away some more.

The law couldn't evade its responsibility any longer. With Mlle. Dio objecting shrilly to Hammerstein's rudeness, and Koster turning treacherously against his partner, the pugilists were carted off to the West 30th Street Police Station. Koster immediately went bail for Kessler, but Hammerstein waited an hour till some friend with cash, learning of his humiliating predicament, arrived to rescue him. In Jefferson Market Court in the morning, Koster and Bial, eager to prove Hammerstein was the villain of the piece, corroborated Kessler's charge that he had been waylaid. Hammerstein denied it, and defended his right to hiss a performer in his own theater. Upholding him, the judge dismissed both men.

Evidently Hammerstein had been scheming for a break. According to one biographer, the three partners bickered endlessly, until the cigar maker began to dream of a house all his own to outshine theirs. He rushed back to the Manhattan Opera and cleaned out his office. In response to his suit, Koster and Bial paid $370,000 cash to get him off their necks. Every penny of it, and much more, would be sunk in an ambitious project to furnish New Yorkers with amusement in the most compact package they had ever enjoyed.

True cosmopolites, these people had always loved a show. An English troupe risked a tour as early as 1732. A playhouse went up in 1758. Before 1800, stock companies began regular appearances, and soon the pleasure-bent public had its choice of two theaters, one, the Park, seating 2000. The Bowery Theater's doors swung wide in 1826. A decade later the count of houses rose to six, all reported well filled every night—were playwrights smarter, or audiences not so smart? By the mid-nineteenth century the bright-lights district blazoned forth in Union Square, with 30 blocks to go to Times Square. From Wallack's Theater, his second, at 13th and Broadway, from the Academy of Music and the Germania, later Tony Pastor's, both at Irving Place and 14th Street, a northward advance set in, and drew the Rialto along in its wake. A headlong surge carried it past Koster and Bial's twin-pillared, five-story opera house on 23rd Street near Sixth Avenue, past the Madison Square Theater west of Broadway on 24th, the Fifth Avenue Theater at Broadway and 28th, the new Wallack's at 30th, the Standard at 35th, the new Metropolitan Opera House at 39th, the Empire Theater at Broadway and 40th, and on the threshold of tomorrow, the Broadway at Broadway and 41st.

Charles Frohman opened the Empire in January 1893, with *The Girl I Left Behind Me*. In 1895 when Frohman titillated New Yorkers with the first of innumerable sophisticated performances of *The Importance of Being Earnest*, Hammerstein stood ready to unveil his Olympia, a five-in-one deal: three halls, roof garden, and café.

Electric lights stopped at 42nd Street, accepted tacitly as the deadline for theaters. But the unorthodox Hammerstein had determined to cross it, and invade the Thieves' Lair, as they called the unsavory Broadway-Seventh Avenue intersection. He appreciated its potentialities as a hub of traffic and population, and besides, felt the utmost confidence in the drawing power of his brand of diversified entertainment; it ought to lure audiences for miles, not merely blocks. For $850,000 he bought eight lots on the east side of Broadway, site of a market and the 71st Regiment headquarters. Adding to this frontage of 203 feet, he pushed back in along the adjacent streets a distance of 154 feet on 45th and 101 on 44th. The bill amounted to more than $1,000,000.

Ground was broken in January 1895, for a unique emporium to cost $600,000. Hammerstein envisaged not just a theater, not just a music hall, but an entire amusement resort, a Crystal Palace of the dramatic arts, or a miniature Times Square all under one roof a decade before anyone had breathed the name Times Square.

Munsey's magazine published a regular feature on the show business. It campaigned against hats the size of cartwheels which blocked the view of the stage. It attacked the high prices of tickets; why pay more for a farce with only eight or ten people in the cast than for an operetta with dozens of singers and dancers?—which seems like a reasonable complaint even with the one costing $1.50 and the other $2. But it had only praise for Hammerstein's grandiose project. The new Olympia "promises to be one of the sights of the metropolis," it declared the month before the curtain, or the five curtains, ran up, and elaborated on the prediction:

"Many new handsome theaters have been put up in New York during the past decade, but little pains has been taken with the exterior effect of any of them. The Olympia, however, is so advantageously situated, where Broadway widens out at 44th Street, that it would have been a pity not to make the most of the opportunity, and this Mr. Hammerstein has done. The front of the structure is of Indiana limestone, supported by pillars of polished granite. Free use is made of ornamental work in the lengthy façade, and yet all is in good taste."

Hammerstein, a better Hammerstein booster even than *Munsey's*, boasted in an advertisement in the *Times* of "the grandest amusement temple in the world," absolutely fireproof and fitted with automatic sprinklers. Two massive carved doorways led to a marble foyer designed to knock out the public eye, and on to a passenger elevator. Four dynamos provided a total of 3200 amperes for lights. Some modern equipment would be involved in a fatal accident the second day.

The Music Hall occupied the 45th Street corner, and the Theater, the 44th, with the Concert Hall in the center. The Music Hall, in red and gold, had eleven tiers of boxes, or 124 in all, more than in any single house in the world, according to the impresario. The chandelier shone blindingly with 600 arc lights. Two pilasters framing the proscenium arch were capped by a cornice with a shield regally bearing the initials OH. Statues and paintings filled the niches and hung on most of the walls. The color scheme of the Theater with 84 boxes or more than the Metropolitan Opera was blue and gold; and of the Concert Hall, cream and gold.

Prices began at 50 cents for standing room in any or all halls, and rose to 75 cents and $1.50 for the Music Hall offering 30 vaudeville artists, and the Theater with 80. The Concert Hall had no reserved seats.

The opening, scheduled for November 18, was changed to November 25; Hammerstein, denying he won a $5000 bet by the postponement, claimed on the contrary that the week's delay cost him $3000. But by all accounts he sold enough extra admissions to cancel that loss and more. The *Times* charged that, with accommodations available for only 6000 patrons, 10,000 paid to get in. To soothe the tempers of these disappointed, not to say deceived, ticket-holders whose rights were usurped flagrantly by early comers, the band in the Concert Hall played on and on to one o'clock in the morning.

Yvette Guilbert, promised for the first night, came to Times Square only in mid-December. The Music Hall presented a singer, a dancer, a skirt dancer, a violinist, a strong man, a female impersonator, a wire artist, aerial gymnasts, triple bar performers, marionettes, acrobats, and, for a macabre feature supposedly as funny as a crutch, a troupe of one-legged acrobatic clowns, all fresh from Europe. The Theater public saw Edward E. Rice's *Excelsior, Jr.*, with Fay Templeton in the title role. Credited with beautiful costumes and settings and described as a tuneful but not a new comic opera, it comprised largely a set of imitations of Buffalo Bill, and an Irish informer with a nose cold, and Paderewski with a sponge as a double-purpose stage property: worn to suggest the pianist's long hair, and then on the floor as a mat to wipe his feet on for his exit.

The *Times,* regarding that house-warming as highly newsworthy, gave it generous space. Though most of those entitled to enter managed to crash into one auditorium or another, a defeated army of an estimated 5000 "slid through the mud and slush of Longacre back into the ranks of Cosmopolis." Hours before curtain time society fashionably dressed assembled in the Square and grew to the dimensions of a mob as cable cars and hansom cabs delivered fresh loads of revelers. They "finally with the strength of a dozen catapults banged at the doors of the new castle of pleasure and sent them flying open." By eight o'clock the masses of people stretched well beyond the tracks, and "puffed sleeves wilted and crimped hair became hoydenish in the crush and the rain; toes were trampled and patent leathers and trousers were splashed, dresses were torn, and still the crowd pushed on."

Inside it was dry, but it was worse.

"Move on, somewhere, ladies and gentlemen!" the desperate ticket taker cried. "Theater to the right, Music Hall to the left; go on!"

Men and women knocked over some brass supports connected by plushed ropes and sprawled across them into a forbidden area.

"Close the doors!" Hammerstein shouted.

But it couldn't be done. An emergency call for extra officers of the law brought twenty who divided in two squads to stop up the breaks in the dike and beat out paths into the Theater and Music Hall. The stairs were impassable. The ushers, however authoritative they looked with their gold epaulettes, had no authority at all and stood by helplessly, while people with flying wedges and around-the-end dashes, but often not with tickets, fought for the boxes. Eventually the police managed three times to shut the doors, but by ten o'clock the crush outside hadn't diminished a bit.

Among those who attended were General Oliver Otis Howard of Civil War fame, Colonel Jacob Ruppert, Jr., Joseph H. Choate, former Lieutenant Governor William F. Sheehan, Congressman Charles G. Conn of Indiana, Elihu Root, and De Lancey Nicoll.

In his last-minute rush, Hammerstein had had a few rooms, in particular private rooms, painted that very day, and some green, red, yellow, and blue still remained wet. Sheehan, excusing himself at intermission, reappeared before his friends with yellow stripes across the back and arms of his dress coat. Nicoll and Root were smeared more festively with yellow, red, and blue. Many of the men's suits were daubed and so, fairly enough, was Hammerstein's. He tried to reassure his public:

"Never mind. It's only water colors. Just look at me. A hand broom will take all that out in the morning."

Down at the Metropolitan Opera House that evening, J. Pierpont Morgan and Mrs. Morgan heard the double bill of Gounod's *Philémon et Baucis* and Mascagni's *Cavalleria Rusticana*. Though Emma Calvé sang Santuzza, the *Times* criticized the performance before a half-empty house as "mild and inoffensive." The return of Daniel Frohman's stock company packed the Lyceum, but not with its habitués, and the observant reviewer wrote:

"It would be gratifying to believe that the absentees had gone to hear Calvé, or even to see the spectacle called *Faust* (an adaptation, at Abbey's Theater). But no, let us be honest. They had all crowded into the Olympia."

Times Square-to-be had launched its theatrical career, and chalked up its noisiest, most crowded and animated night yet. This celebration in effect added Times Square to New York City.

Hammerstein's Broadway site, besides its association with the shady characters who frequented the Thieves' Lair, had had a history marred with ill omens. They included two disastrous fires in the 71st Regiment headquarters; in one, an explosion blew out a plate-glass window and killed a messenger boy. A worse tragedy occurred within twelve hours of the Olympia gala.

After the show or shows, some employees, tuckered out with the excitement and the extra work, visited a nearby barroom for the relief they felt entitled to. Whether this indulgence was as harmless and irrelevant as the management righteously pretended, something went wrong and they were not at their posts at the fatal moment in the morning when a pipe joint burst in the cellar. A steam fitter and a papier-mâché worker were tumbled to their deaths in the pit under the driving wheel, and ten others suffered agonizing scalds. Steam billowed up through gratings in the walk and tortured cries alerted passers-by. Ambulances from Bellevue, Roosevelt, Flower, Hudson Street, New-York and Presbyterian hospitals rushed up at the gallop. Some pitiable victims, with their faces, chests, arms or hands seared red, and ribbons of flesh dangling from them excruciatingly, received first aid across the street in the Olympia Pharmacy.

A union leader charged, "Oscar Hammerstein was just too parsimonious to put that job in the hands of master steam fitters." The impresario retorted that he would keep possession of the blown pipe and exhibit it only to the proper persons. Three were arrested, but freed.

It was a portent. The Olympia, with its awesome pillared entrance and twin towers, proved too expensive. Only an uninterrupted succession of sure-fire hits in every auditorium would pay the bills, and even Hammerstein couldn't pick money-makers infallibly. A run of flops robbed him of control in 1897, and in 1898 bankrupted him. Practically penniless, he forced his way into quarters legally barred to him to recover $400 in cash that he had hidden under a pillow. An undoubted intrinsic value existed in his land. He had refused $6000 annual rental for each Broadway corner for a drugstore and a haberdashery. The entire building sold at auction to New York Life Insurance for $967,000; Henry Sire and M. L. Sire bought it, though stripped of furniture, stage properties and drapes, for more than $1,000,000; Klaw & Erlanger took over for $1,900,000; and in 1920 a department store offered $6,000,000; it was razed in 1935.

Though Hammerstein had exhausted his resources, except of course for the magic of his name and the income from his patents, and couldn't be sure, especially after his initial setback, that the crossroads would justify his extravagant dreams, he still burned with the Times Square fever. Benefits organized for him by his stars netted $8000. By the sort of manipulation only financiers can understand and get away with, he parlayed this modest stake into his next theater, the Victoria, two blocks off at 42nd Street and Seventh Avenue. For a cut-rate construction job costing a mere $80,000, he used secondhand bricks and lumber and even adapted with little change the hayloft of the market stable which had stood there. At his fashionable opening in March 1899, the public-gone-mad paid up to $100 a ticket. Show folks who had christened his Olympia "the Cornerstone of Times Square" labeled this simply "the Corner." Hammerstein's son Willie, a first-rate theater talent, managed it while the irrepressible father went on to build the Republic Theater one door west, on the site of the ill famed McGory's Dance Hall. Across the top of the two of them he laid out the Paradise Roof Gardens. After a circus introduced this stellar attraction in the summer of 1900, it developed in its day into the one New York spot at which visitors felt obliged to spend a night. The underline of a photo identifying the Gardens as "the beginning of Times Square" contains a modicum of truth.

Wonderfully ingenious in their field, the Hammersteins took a chance on a fantastic variety of vaudeville numbers. The "Vegetable Twins," the Cherry Sisters Effie and Addie, appeared at the Olympia in an act which enraged the audience to the point of throwing things. In effect Oscar Hammerstein invited it to, for he arranged for these tedious innocents to play behind a net which intercepted cabbages, oranges, and other missiles. Willie at the Victoria featured two-headed freaks, and a palm reader. Almost nude figures, piously condemned by the church, sneaked past the law under titles meant to clothe them with respectability, such as "Living art studies" and "Reproductions of famous statuary."

Transferred to more traditional and perhaps more dignified ownership, the Olympia divided into the New York Theater and the Criterion Theater, where Julia Marlowe starred in *Barbara Frietchie*, William Faversham in *A Royal Rival*, and Ethel, Jack, and Lionel Barrymore in Barrie plays. Otis Skinner, William Gillette, Mrs. Fiske, Julia Sanderson, Marie Dressler, and Isadora Duncan all strutted their stuff on that stage.

While still the Olympia and still Hammerstein's property, the unique entertainment resort inspired *Munsey's* to fulsome compliments:

"Olympia is all that the name implies, the abode of the gods, if we reckon these, as we are mostly inclined to do nowadays, as presiding over the haunts of pleasure."

When the famous impresario added his elaborate roof garden, a rival to the six already catering to the merrymaking city, the magazine gushed about "an urban fairy-land," which "boasts two ponds, as many rustic bridges, a grotto, several live swans, a monkey and skilful imitations of rocky landscape."

"Its glass top," *Munsey's* also remarked, was "by no means the most novel feature."

But it was a queer glass roofing, just the same, for water streamed over it steadily to cool the air for the customers.

Thus there is nothing new under the sun. Right where the Olympia stood, Regal Shoes, Loft's Candy Shop, Woolworth's, the King of Slims tie shop, the Criterion movie house, and a Bond Clothing Store now do business at street level. Towering above them all is the immense Pepsi-Cola waterfall.

VI "Times Square Is the Name of the City's New Centre"

In the presence of a few dignitaries and the curious who even then flocked to any uncommon event, curly-headed Iphigene Bertha Ochs, eleven years old, pronounced the traditional phrase:

"I declare this stone to be laid plumb, level, and square."

Thus at 3 P.M., Monday, January 18, 1904, the cornerstone of the New York *Times* tower was fixed everlastingly in place at the south edge of the Broadway entrance. The paper, though usually acting on the natural assumption that its own business was news, classified this as a family affair and printed the story inside.

The child, the daughter of *Times* publisher Adolph S. Ochs and Mrs. Iphigene Ochs, took merely the first step in a journalistic career; she would marry Arthur Hays Sulzberger, who succeeded his father-in-law as publisher. After she smoothed out the mortar, and the stone was lowered the last couple of feet, she gave it three symbolic taps with her silver trowel. According to the Springfield *Republican,* she performed the rite "with a charming grace," and as competently as a regular mason. Bishop Henry C. Potter, who offered prayer, shook her little hand.

71

Ochs' editor Charles R. Miller delivered the principal speech.

For that season, the midafternoon temperature was tolerable, and the brief program closed before bitter cold swept over the city in the evening.

Five feet long and half as high and thick, the stone contained copies of the *Times,* the Chattanooga *Times* from which Ochs had climbed the ladder to New York, and fifteen other newspapers; photographs and biographies of the two architects, C. L. W. Eidlitz and Andrew C. MacKenzie; a World Almanac and a Who's Who; and the program, including Miller's florid oration—the cluttered top of any city-room desk would yield a similar varied, nondescript, black-and-white harvest.

In less than twelve months this aspirant skyscraper welcomed its numerous occupants, but much sooner, in less than three, it suggested a different name for the familiar Longacre intersection. As a man from Germany was "father" of Times Square, a man from Cincinnati and son of a man from Germany, nine years Hammerstein's junior and of his religious faith, became godfather and contributed the designation "Times Square" which Mayor Robert F. Wagner later regarded as "synonymous with New York."

Adolph S. Ochs, born in 1858, worked as a newsboy in Knoxville, according to the Horatio Alger formula, and began his rapid rise in Chattanooga where a pistol-packing brother scared off offended readers, one of whom once drew a gun on Adolph himself. In 1896 he bought the New York *Times,* and was almost too smart about enlarging its circulation and advertising revenue, for he crowded it right out of its old Park Row house and home. Tempted by

downtown sites, as Charles Frohman was, he considered Broadway at Barclay Street, where the Woolworth Building soars massively to 60 stories. But like Hammerstein he had the imagination to guess at the uptown center's unprecedented potentialities. The first electric trolley already ran the length of 42nd Street, selected as a main thoroughfare on the 1811 Randall map. Ground was broken near City Hall for the first subway—people liked to call it "tunnel" but contractor John B. MacDonald preferred "trench" as technically correct—which would follow Lexington to 42nd, switch over to Longacre Square by the present shuttle route, swing with screeching wheels around a sharp curve and thunder on up Broadway. Ochs decided to bet on the northward trend, and in 1902 just before sailing for Europe with his family, signed up for the three-sided plot for his *Times* Tower.

Some people trying to picture that crossroads before the *Times* moved in might imagine a simple Grover's Corners, the tracks going this way, the row of hitching posts, the drugstore and the soda fountain. Historians of the paper haven't taken much pains to dispel this notion, either, perhaps because the more they depreciate the mushrooming area, the more credit the *Times* gets for developing it. But it had lost forever its pristine rural aspect, and it had been years since the chickens went to roost at this spot and the cows came home. Hammerstein had inaugurated his imposing Olympia with its unmistakably citified look; and opposite it across Broadway a substantial four-story apartment, the Barrington, stretched trim lines of awnings above the walk. The Victoria and Republic plus the single roof garden surmounting them drew capacity crowds. The several stores and private school which long occupied the

Times site gave way to a nine-story building, also decorated with awnings, where about 1890 an Irish innkeeper named Regan started a bar and restaurant he called a rathskeller. By the time Ochs concluded his deal, it had grown into the thriving Pabst Hotel and Restaurant. At this same bustling period the Astor Hotel was going up, the Cadillac was up, the Knickerbocker would quickly replace the St. Cloud, and the Lew M. Fields Theater, Hammerstein's eighth, opened farther west on 42nd Street. The Public Library lay only five years off and two blocks east.

Ochs' parcel of land points north, as does the Flatiron Building lot a mile away. Both have been compared to ships breasting the Broadway current. Pabst, on the contrary, faced not the future city but the old, for its elaborate glassed-in, gingerbread entrance stood on 42nd Street to greet customers, most of whom arrived from the south. The *Times* put a door in the same spot; but for its main one with columns flanking it and miniature balcony, perhaps for lack of space on the narrow uptown edge, it chose the east or longest side. Here little Iphigene officiated.

Overhead, the last stone to the left in the tier directly beneath the running news sign bears the name Charles Thorley. Real estate man, Tammany politician, owner of the lease, and avid for a footnote in history, he stipulated in the contract that the letters be cut there.

Just another kibitzer, Ochs frequently hired a room in the Cadillac at Broadway and 43rd Street so he could peer down on his mammoth construction job and gloat over its progress. Tourists and natives, too, gaped down into the jagged excavation blasted out of rock, "deepest and biggest hole in the city," as a rival journal ruefully admitted, illuminated fearsomely like a Gustave Doré inferno. Workers pushing the subway through at the same time nearly flooded themselves out when they tapped a Styx which the Great Kill should have drained. It was the beginning of the removal of incalculable quantities of stone and dirt to make room for not only subway and building foundations but also water pipes, steam pipes, sewage lines, and an unbelievable tangle of wires till the whole Square was hollowed out beneath a thin envelope of paving.

The *Times* dug down 55 feet below street level to imbed its presses at the very bottom, even below the subway—by which the astute Ochs would ship papers to Brooklyn at least as fast as the competitors who counted on beating him since they operated on Park Row right off the end of the Brooklyn Bridge. Now that the *Times* has moved to 43rd Street, Hotaling stores his out-of-town newspapers in this ancient, silent cavern.

August Belmont, third man of German descent to play a lead role in building up this intersection, headed the Interborough Rapid Transit Company. In that capacity he addressed a plea to Alexander E. Orr, president of the Board of Rapid Transit Commissioners:

'The Interborough Rapid Transit Company desires very much to characterize, so far as it can, its important distributing stations by name, where other converging transportation lines make such a station a centre, or, if for any reason, it is in the neighborhood of some conspicuous institution, like Columbia College"—Belmont sounded a little incoherent with excitement, or wasn't so good at sentences as at subways.

"No station on our route is liable to be more active or

important than that at Forty-Second Street and Broadway. We are planning, in connection with the Times Building, to have access to it from Seventh Avenue. Owing to the conspicuous position which the *Times* holds, it being one of the leading New York journals, it would seem fitting that the Square on which its building stands should be known as Times Square, and the station named Times Station. Long Acre, the present name of the Square, means nothing, and is not generally known throughout the city."

Beverley R. Robinson, for the Times Square district, sponsored this letter in the Board of Aldermen. A resolution carrying the idea into effect, after indorsement by the Commission of Streets, Highways and Sewers, was approved unanimously in two votes. It passed definitively on April 13, 1904. The signature of Mayor George B. McClellan on April 19 brought into formal existence one of the few place names almost universally known in the Western Hemisphere.

If a visitor or even a native can't bound the Square today, it may be because most of the originators were themselves confused. Of two latter-day historians of the *Times,* one sets the Square's southern limit at 43rd Street, and the other, Meyer Berger, who is correct, at 42nd. Belmont's letter referred indecisively to "the territory heretofore known as Long Acre Square." The aldermen, though they described it on three occasions, hit it exactly right only once. The *Times* was accurate as far as it went. In a story captioned "Times Square Is the Name of City's New Centre," it claimed, reducing Longacre to one word, that "Times Square takes in the triangle on which the new building of the New York *Times* is situated, and the name applies to the entire section." This would become, Ochs predicted more wisely than he ever dreamed, an "international crossroads."

Understandably vain, the newspaper jumped the gun. Already on April 9, days before the mayor legalized the change, it was complacently editorializing. Pointing out that the subway station couldn't very well be called either 42nd Street or Broadway, since those thoroughfares ran on endlessly, it reflected:

"The name Times Station naturally suggested itself since the subway passed through the first underground story of the Times Building, and as the building which the *Times* has under construction is the most conspicuous edifice in that part of the city and gives character to it, that fact is appropriately recognized in the adoption of the name Times Square.

"Very likely the name would have been conferred by the speech of the people without official action. The action of the city authorities gives legal sanction to the name Times Square. It is a name that serves perfectly for identification and is one, we think, not likely to be forgotten in this community."

The Times Building rose 375 feet, then the second highest in New York, and counting basements and sub-basements, the highest. Besides its location, size was its chief claim to fame. A handsome modernized structure, to be sure, it has been praised as Giotto's Tower, New York style. Actually the architects did no more than copy the outlines and proportions of the Pabst Hotel and Restaurant, a soaring tower on the 42nd Street side but truncated at the northern point—much as the pair of architects for the Crystal Palace had supinely imitated the design of Sir Joseph Paxton of London. Eidlitz and MacKenzie just tore

79

down and put up bigger, and their handiwork was more Pabst than Giotto. But Ochs had undoubted advantages to celebrate. The paper advertised its situation as "close to termini" of half a dozen railroads, and near 49 hotels, 17 theaters, seven bank and trust companies, and 12 leading clubs. It listed the weight of the steel at 3000 tons, and boasted of the granite base, the sedate facings of terra cotta and brick, the elevators with safety devices, and vacuum cleaning throughout. The *Times* would occupy the tower and the underground space, and rent 12 stories.

Formal opening and dedication occurred at New Year's. On the last day of the year, Ochs managed the complicated transfer of his heavy presses and other equipment from Park Row to the uptown quarters, to print there the next day. An enormous crowd gathered to see 1904 out and 1905 in. Fanciulli's Band tootled away on a stand on the 43rd Street side. The fun-loving public brought horns, whistles, rattles, and cruder noise-makers like resined strings to pull shrilly through tin cans. Many cab and auto parties arrived. From ten o'clock on every restaurant had to turn away well-dressed people. Berger said "hundreds of thousands" came to "witness a brilliant fireworks display touched off in the tower." He continued:

"Midtown skies reverberated with the thunderous bursting of flights of bombs. Skyrockets and flares streaked against the midnight sky in the first Times Square New Year's Eve show, centered around the tower. Those assemblages became traditional with *Times* electricians controlling incandescent figures that spelled out the dying year and spelled in the new. The signal for the old year's passing was a massive illuminated globe that slid down the tower pole while the crowds far below on the sidewalk cut loose with ear-splitting din. A final burst of fireworks wrote 1905 in flame against the heavens, and the throngs screamed and shouted themselves hoarse. It was one of the greatest promotion projects of the age. The idea was Ochs'. He knew the value of such advertising."

Berger the historian exercised a literary restraint which the feverish *Times* itself scorned in its lead story of January 1, 1905. Speaking of the fireworks, it exulted:

"No more beautiful picture was ever limned in fire on the curtain of midnight. From the four corners of the skyscraper lambent flames played. From base to dome the giant structure was alight—a torch to usher in the new born, a funeral pyre for the old which pierced the very heavens."

You might suspect editor Miller wrote this, for he had delivered an equally effusive address at the laying of the cornerstone:

"The shadow of these walls, with the coming and departing suns, shall fall upon uncounted myriads of men, whose tread shall echo round them, whose eyes shall become wonted to their harmonious proportions, and whose voices shall swell the note and hum of the busy city through generation after generation until where we now stand a gray and time-stained pile shall stir the passer-by to reverie by its venerable and historic interest."

This ostentatious prose, it was decided by some one, shall not be *Times* style today, nor anywhere near Times Square style. But underneath the stilted verbiage lay a vision, blurred perhaps but unmistakable, of future prospects. No doubt the wish was father to the thought, but the thought would be corroborated. The *Times* suggested the erection on its topmost roof of an immense sign for carriage calls for patrons of the neighborhood theaters. Thus, it said, "the plaza (as it called the Square) would become the real centre of midnight activities."

Other immense signs, whole walls and cliffs of them, shine down now on that plaza till midnight has become its brightest hour.

VII "Show me any other industry that has done so much for Broadway"

SAIL THE SEAS OF PASSION AND VIOLENCE WITH THE BOLD-EST WARRIORS THE WORLD HAS EVER KNOWN

This perfervid exhortation invited the public to a movie two or three blocks up from the *Times*. Flashing above the Square in blinding seven-foot letters, it extended over 200 feet in a straight line; the designer and manufacturer, who believed that news fit to print should be printed whopping big, boasted of it as "the longest running single sign ever made."

In part it was the *Times'* prophecy of a hub of midnight activities come true. But it also explains to a degree why not one legitimate theater any longer faces on the Square itself.

The film, *The Vikings*, played in two houses side by side, Astor and Victoria. The monster sign rearing above the double façade showed a Viking boat three times larger than any the Vikings themselves ever launched, with 11 motor-driven sweeps 16 feet long that pulled back and forth in unison, a 50-foot mast and a real sail sewn up by real sailmakers—or enough power with a stiff breeze to up-anchor the building itself and send it scudding along

Broadway. Above that, Kirk Douglas, Tony Curtis, Ernest Borgnine, and Janet Leigh, variously bearded, bushy, coiffed, and crowned as on the screen, looked out upon the world from 38-foot portraits.

Below them, along the walks and the safety island still wet after a shower, an impatient crowd stirred within the niggardly space measured off by the police and their wooden barriers. Though taxis delivered many patrons and guests, a whole train of shiny black limousines half as big as railroad cars came whispering to the curb. The uniformed chauffeurs hopped out, flung the rear doors wide, doffed their visored caps, and bowed out the celebrities. A woman from the producer's office mounted watch at the Astor entrance and like a butler announced the great and near great; only the poor nobodies passed without filmland accolade. Whoever she identified turned with professional alacrity toward the waiting cameras, flash bulbs lighted up the man's white shirt front and the woman's gown and bottomless cleavage, and then they disappeared inside.

The sophisticated crowd didn't need tips:

"It's Tony Curtis!"

"Hi-ya, Tony!"

"Lookit, Janet Leigh!"

The public cheered Kirk Douglas. A new cry sounded:

"H'ray, Steve Allen!"

Accompanied by his wife Jayne Meadows, he responded with a wave and a smile.

A bus stopping where it cut off the view drew a few gibes. Some one remarked:

"Anyways, see it all better on TV."

Curtain time meant that the notables had reported in and been counted, and the cops swung harshly into action:

"That's all! Break it up!"

The fans retreated docilely, except for one sarcastic rejoinder:

"That's all? Don't they come out?"

The sad day finally arrived when the legitimate actor and actress never did come out of the Broadway doors again. The last of the regular big-time vaudeville shows on Broadway or Seventh Avenue between 42nd and 47th Streets seems to have been at Loew's State on December 23, 1947, when 26 years of continuous vaudeville in that house ended. Straight theater, with a maximum of eight performances a week, vying with movies which cater to three times as many audiences, had long ago surrendered ignominiously in the battle for these de luxe premises. Actually the theater here was doomed from the start, for aggressive filmdom threatened even its earliest insecure footholds.

Edison patented his Kinetoscope in 1891, four years before Hammerstein opened the Olympia. The Kinetoscope Parlor exhibiting flickering 50-foot reels of Buffalo Bill and Annie Oakley dated from 1894. The public got its first fresh taste of film at Koster and Bial's in April 1896, when the Vitascope ground out a rudimentary entertainment in three acts: two blond dancers, angry surf, and burlesque of a boxing match. Vaudeville programs began to add the popular one-reelers in 1899.

Adolph Zukor had invested in an arcade in 14th Street at Broadway, where Ohrbach's would stand. The entrepreneurs ripped out a restaurant that extended clear through to 13th Street, redecorated, and installed one hundred peep shows. Everything in those good old days cost a penny—to enter, look, listen to phonograph records, eat a

87

bite, drink a soda and try the shooting gallery in the basement. The sign in lights read:

AUTOMATIC ONE CENT VAUDEVILLE

Daily take amounted to $500 or $700, or up to 14,000 customers if they blew a nickel apiece. Then in 1904 the novice impresarios, Zukor and his partners, converted rooms overhead to Crystal Hall for that rampaging modern medium, the film. Zukor also planned a street-level place nearby but his associates were leery of the competition; as he later remarked, they should have learned about the theaters packed in Times Square today. Zukor interested Daniel Frohman in his first full-length silent-screen offering, Sarah Bernhardt in *Queen Elizabeth*, and the press and a few guests viewed it on another memorable date, in July 1912.

The first house designed exclusively for movies, the Strand, on Broadway at 47th at the northern extremity of the Square, opened in 1914 with Rex Beach's *The Spoilers*. In the same year the Criterion, part of Hammerstein's Olympia, shifted from live shows to the Hollywood product. In 1927 the Warner Theater billed the first evening-long talkie.

Other conventional theaters appeared, though even before the roof was on, filmdom came knocking doggedly for admittance: the New Theater (later the Century) on Central Park West, the Little Theater in 44th Street, the Henry Miller in 43rd, the Astor, Winter Garden, the Times Square, the Apollo. New construction ceased. The Paramount, at 33 stories the Square's tallest building, dates from 1926. Occasionally it billed a crooner. Frank Sinatra's press agent hired a dozen girls to scream or swoon when he sang there. By dawn of opening day, 10,000 teen-agers had queued up to crash the doors, they reduced 320 special police to a helpless dither, and screamed and swooned all over absolutely for free. At New Year's, 1958, rock 'n' roller Alan Freed attracted 11,000 zany teen-agers, numbering four girls to one boy. They threatened to stomp the floor down inside, though out, the forehanded police erected wooden horses to protect plate glass all around the block. But for its main dish, this city skyscraper with its village chimes and three-story clock presents films, as do its neighbors the Criterion, Astor, Victoria, Loew's State, Palace, Forum, and Rialto.

In the midtown amusement district, people naïve and innocent once paid to see Otis Skinner, William Gillette, Julia Sanderson, Isadora Duncan, John Drew, Maude Adams, Blanche Bates, Mrs. Patrick Campbell, Olga Nethersole, David Warfield, Al Jolson, Elsie Janis; to see the *Florodora* girls, the *Sorceress, Peter Pan, When Knighthood Was in Flower, A Grand Army Man, Ben-Hur, Chantecler, The Constant Wife, The Kingdom of God, Trilby.*

Turning next to movies, they paid to see a girl shinny up an apple tree, a tramp steal a pie, an impish boy set fire to grouchy grandpa's paper, a wife catch her husband kissing his stenographer, a servant spill food down the necks of guests in evening clothes.

Nowadays the crowds along 42nd Street and up Seventh Avenue and Broadway pay to see "Boris Karloff, King of Monsters," in *Haunted Strangler,* or *Fiend Without Face,* called a "Brutal Story of Young Girls." In case this doesn't lure the boys in flashy sweaters, the girls with tinted eyelids and skin-tight slacks, the unclean-minded old men with a beady stare, the girls with girls and the boys with boys, an advertising poster shrieks in large type:

"We guarantee it will shock you."

Or Elvis Presley plays in *King Creole*: "A young New Orleans entertainer fights his way to the top against hoodlums, gangs and their girl bait. . . . His blood has never been so hot. His songs have never been so cool." There he postures in a photo to prove it, with the curling lip and the brassy gleam in his eye.

Other signs are scandalous decoys: ELYSIA: VALLEY OF NUDES, MISS BODY BEAUTIFUL, SUPER-SONIC HELL CREATURE, BOMBSHELL, EXPLOSIVE, FIENDISH, FRENZIED, BLOOD CHILLING.

Adolph Zukor, confidently assessing the accomplishments of Hollywood and the film business in general, issued this challenge:

"Show me any other industry that has done so much for Broadway."

VIII "Pity the sky
with nothing
but stars"

The mammoth electric signs which make Times Square the burning core of the bright-lights district started out little and just grew, though it has been said that an advertising man, O. J. Gude, first suggested them. He also proposed calling Broadway the Great White Way—George White of *Scandals* fame liked to joke that it was named for him.

New Yorkers began to advertise about as early as they had a wall on which to hang a sign. Anyone with something to sell nailed a notice over his door, slung it from a beam above his sidewalk, or painted the word for his product on the pavement—"Zozodont," in one spot under foot, and in another, ominous and mystifying, "Blood." The cutlery shop announced its whereabouts with a huge dummy pair of scissors; the undertaker, with a tombstone. The locksmith set out gilded wooden keys and saws, and other specialty clienteles were summoned with the images of gun, awl, head with or without teeth, cigar, pipe, horseshoe, pen, a bust of Beethoven and, as one visitor mocked, "a modeled human foot the size of a cab horse" at the chiropodist's. One music store outlined a large harp in tiny flames.

A gas mantle was invented by Baron Carl Auer von Welsbach, and street lamps crept single-file up Broadway in the 1880s and '90s. Already electricity wired and domesticated was the inventor's gift to the advertiser. Georges Claude would develop neon tubing and introduce it to Times Square only in the 1920s, but a quarter century before, incandescent bulbs in straight rows of dots defined stiffly the edges of store fronts and ran up and over and down the façades of theaters, or picked out of the dark such trade-marks as the famous griffin at Rector's restaurant.

In the lighted sign, "Crystal Palace," which Zukor erected in 1904 over his peep show and movie, each letter consisted of about ten bulbs—one thousand bulbs, or one hundred times as many, illuminate each one of the nine letters of the "Budweiser" whose beams now shine down Broadway almost a mile. If that display forecast Times Square, an inside installation provided a much gaudier preview. To mount to the second floor from the penny arcade, Zukor enclosed the stairs in a glass shell; water within it cascaded over lights of different colors. This creation probably had to be seen to be believed, but it already hinted at the flaring, sparkling nighttime Times Square of today.

It is the sudden darkness, not the light but its absence, experts say, which draws our glance; solid lights show far, but turned on intermittently they attract attention much quicker. Furthermore, they are more fun moving than still, and cost decidedly less to operate.

The first outsize electric sign appeared where the

Flatiron Building stands, but on what was then a nine-story structure. It proclaimed the advantages of Sapolio and Spencerian steel pens. A larger display replaced it: MANHATTAN BEACH SWEPT BY OCEAN BREEZES. In this Square, too, the public read election returns projected by stereopticon.

By the start of this century, producers and managers in the entertainment field, and some business leaders, also, suspected the newfangled lights would mean money in their pockets. Maxine Elliott was the first actress to have her name spelled out in bulbs on her theater at 39th Street. The pioneering "spectacular," as show people designated the flashing signs, celebrated the *Florodora* girls around 1900; the sextette agleam in carbon filaments in a grid of wire like a giant toaster sashayed back and forth in a simulated dance step above the Casino Theater on the corner of Broadway and 39th Street.

Zoning laws adopted in 1916 granted Times Square and Broadway special dispensations in the size and brilliance of outdoor displays. The building code imposed safety regulations, of course; no aerial framework could over-balance its base. Otherwise the sky was the limit—the sky of which a Frenchman exclaimed lyrically:

"Pity the sky with nothing but stars."

The result is two Times Squares, the bustling intersection by day, crowded, noisy, blunt but recognizable as part and parcel of the metropolis, and by night the frisky quarter of razzledazzle and fantastic flummery, not Bohemia, not Left Bank, not circus, side show, midway, or fair but uniquely Times Square. A Mazda mecca, its phenomenal illumination is visible fifty miles at sea, a "sulphur glow," as Ninette de Valois extolled it, "a kindled alphabet" in the evocative words of Paul Morand. What an enjoyable place, Jules Romains imagined, if it had a few sidewalk cafés! G. K. Chesterton declared:

"How beautiful it would be for some one who could not read!"

For those who do read, it is a bazaar, and they are invited, or constrained, to sample a boundless variety of goods and services proffered in the script of bulb and neon tubing: legitimate theater, movie, radio and TV, naturally, and also hotels, corsets, candy, soft, medium-hard and hard drinks, autos, peanuts, newspapers, magazines, a novel, travel, furniture, cigarettes, airlines, shoes, pens, pencils, frankfurters, cleansing tissues, irons, typewriters, cocoa, coffee, gum, crackers, tires, toothpaste, soap, air conditioning.

The lights draw an audience of an incalculable size so that the Square, center of the theater district, has become itself a theater, grandest of them all, with the SRO sign always out. A Frenchman praised it as "the finest free show on earth." Even the artful phrases devised by the designers of spectaculars assume that they work on a stage. Artkraft Strauss claims, "The commercial is the show"; Douglas Leigh refers to his contrivances as "electricks." One of their employees, who checks for burned-out bulbs, boasts: "It's my show, and I keep it going. I guarantee all my stars a long run." A visitor declared: "Somewhere behind the scenes there is a marvelously gifted producer."

Artkraft Strauss and Leigh are the principal sign makers. Leigh, Alabama banker's son, has sailed 12-inch soap bubbles across Times Square, sent up steam in clouds from a cyclopean cup of coffee, puffed cigarette smoke rings into

the air, and constructed the biggest waterfall on the island of Manhattan.

He entered the University of Florida but quit after two years, $10,000 richer thanks to his supersalesmanship. An advertising job for the St. Moritz established him in New York; for this, the hotel paid him $50 a month, and let him use a two-room suite for a year. From these impressive headquarters he launched his successful campaign for Times Square frontage.

The oldest firm is Artkraft Strauss, dating from 1897. The president is Russian-born Jacob Starr; the trade shortens it to Jake. In his native land he studied to be an electrician; and as a youngster helped set up the name of his school in electric lights. Arriving in America in 1907, he waited three years to meet Ben Strauss, then the head of a company which did a small business for David Belasco, Al Jolson, and Klaw & Erlanger producing cards and posters, humble antecedents of quarter-million-dollar signs. Starr, who weighed 98 pounds, applied to Strauss ambitiously for a husky fellow's job, and was hired as blacksmith. From 1928 on he ran his own business for six years, and then resumed the Strauss association. Artkraft Strauss officials believe in a 16-hour day, that is, for themselves. In their opinion, and in their line, a mechanic doesn't amount to much unless he is also electrician, welder, plumber, riveter, engineer, and sheet-metal worker, able to build as well as operate drills, presses, and lathes. The Artkraft Strauss shop on Twelfth Avenue in the shadow of the elevated highway also employs glass blowers and artists. They are full-fledged, academy-trained artists, of course, though they swing a brush no less than four inches wide, dipped in a palette with twelve compartments each of which holds half a pint of color. When, after the long-hair fashion, the Artkraft Strauss painter wants to step back to examine his handiwork in the proper perspective, he may have to climb down 50 or 75 feet to street level and back way across Times Square.

Artkraft Strauss's normal staff of two hundred includes half-a-dozen sign watchers, who parade the crossroads and adjacent Broadway all evening long to make sure no fuse blows and no figure vanishes out of the bright sky— two hundred to three hundred burned-out single bulbs have to be replaced every 24 hours by daytime crews. Youngsters expert at typing are stationed in a control box hidden on some rooftop. Kleenex, Admiral, TWA, Budweiser, and some others, for instance, all operate from one shack behind the Palace. The attendant changes words in the traveling lines as quickly as he can tap them out on teletype.

"You have to be a bit pixie in this business," Jake Starr's son Melvin confessed.

A prankish atmosphere surrounds it. When a major advertiser lands in town, Starr may insert a welcome to him in the message moving ceaselessly beneath the ad for which his company foots the bill. The VIP looks up and to his astonishment reads in 10-foot letters: "Howdy, Mr. Doakes." Since presumably almost any man alive would give his shirt to see his name in lights on Broadway, this no doubt sends Mr. Doakes on the run to enter into a perpetual contract with Artkraft Strauss.

Part of his gratification, of course, is the realization that thousands of others see his name, too. Just how many thousands, no one knows. A check at successive corners would catch a lot of noses twice. One 24-hour tally added up to 90,000 passers-by; with 32 corners from 42nd Street to 47th, excluding those without buildings, the total would be 2,880,000. No one pretends it's that big, but the claims, mostly blind guesses, do not jibe.

Richard C. Patterson, Jr., commissioner of the Department of Commerce and Public Events, contributes the official figure of 13,000,000 a week.

"No such habitual concourse of multitudes can be seen anywhere else in the world," said one writer correctly, though carefully not providing an actual count; London's Piccadilly with a daily population of 500,000 is runner-up. According to a smart but generalized prophecy by Horatio Seymour, governor of New York during the Civil War, Broadway "was destined to be trodden by more people than ever migrated through any other avenue of travel on the globe."

The Square proper may attract 10,000,000 every week. Police believe half a million squeeze in for a special celebration, plus 100,000 in the side streets. Advertisers with space to sell can be relied on absolutely: they never belittle the size of the audience. They express their claims in several forms, direct and roundabout:

The *Time-Life-Sports Illustrated* display is credited with three quarters of a million daily viewers. Or the former Budweiser sign, where the TWA plane now almost buzzes Toffenetti's restaurant, cost less than a twentieth of a cent per impression per person. Or nightly visitors equalled the combined population of Atlanta and San Francisco. Or Canadian Club has two and a half million candle power, the equivalent of two candle power for every passer-by every twenty-four hours.

The north end broadens out into the most advantageous

spot for a display, and crowds of hundreds of thousands, indeed millions, are reminded incessantly of beer by the illuminated Budweiser up Broadway at 49th Street—there is nothing subtle or subliminal about Times Square advertising. Three of the most theatrical spectaculars, however, the plane, the Pepsi-Cola waterfall and the Kleenex, are mounted nearer the south end.

Sometimes Artkraft Strauss designers turn out over two dozen sketches in the search for one that strikes their fancy. Then they project it on the board, trace or copy it and enlarge its original 8 by 10 inches to cover as much as 2000 square feet. Little Lulu hops around the vast Kleenex display by means of 32 separate copies of her in acetate, each one then cut out in neon tubing. The hand which darts down to pull tinted Kleenex tissue out of the box is viewed in six different positions. The plausible realism with which the Budweiser eagle flaps its wings results from six momentary exposures—it's the old flicker technique. The six horses jogging along with the wagon and beer barrels required 48 different drawings.

One on top of the other five advertisements—new ones keep coming up, of course—separate Broadway and Seventh Avenue at the two exits, or entrances, at 47th Street: Castro Convertible furniture for the store at ground level, and Hit Parade cigarettes, both stills; above them, three spectaculars, in ascending order, Admiral Television Appliances, Canadian Club Imported Whisky, and at the summit, bracketing its rivals with messages traveling vertically on the left and right, or west and east edges, Chevrolet.

Admiral's green border does not move, its white does; it shines with the artificial colors of stick candy like peppermint, raspberry, and wintergreen, and the lights work by a ceaseless on-again off-again on-again system. Covering two square rods, it takes a whole minute to reel off its repertory of 50 effects without repeating. Artkraft Strauss regards it proudly as "the most flexible sign ever built."

TWA stages a "show" 100 feet long by 75 high, brain child of the airline's art director Rex Werner and product of the Artkraft Strauss shop. The plane duplicates a Super Constellation, fully round, scaled to a little over a third actual size, the fuselage 46 feet, the wing span 48, or larger than the Wrights' at Kitty Hawk. It is structurally stronger, or more rigid, than the real machine because it must stand a variety of strains without give.

Douglas Leigh originally contrived the Pepsi-Cola spectacular for Bond Clothes, with a pair of giants, male and female, their chests thrown out in the best physical-education manner, posted like sentinels where the bottles now glint. It stretches for an entire block along the east side of Broadway and around the corners of 44th and 45th Streets, where Hammerstein cooled the glass top of his roof garden. Its million watts could have lighted Ebbets Field for a night game. The two bottles, five stories high, are called the largest ever made; to fill them would take a million eight-ounce bottles of the popular beverage. Heard above some traffic sounds below, water plunges over the brink at the rate of 50,000 gallons a minute. This requires a supply of 10,000 gallons used over and over again; 3000 gallons of anti-freeze stave off trouble in cold weather. A vacuum system has been devised to keep strong winds from whisking vagrant drops away.

One sign possessed the special virtue of dispensing with

lights. When the wartime blackout forced the manufacturer to attract attention to his wares without the aid of kilowatts, Leigh produced his Camel Cigarettes advertisement, an "electrick" without electricity. The features of some eminent movie star, theater idol, or baseball player are painted on the wall where Rector's restaurant once lured society folks, and the O-shaped mouth blows 15 smoke rings a minute—steam from Con Edison pipes—above the heads of the marveling pedestrians. The spieler in the sight-seeing bus jokes to his passengers:

"He's never coughed yet."

The block-long sign for the film, *The Vikings*, though it didn't last a whole season, cost $100,000 to erect and get into operation, according to Melvin Starr. The Pepsi-Cola was classed as a half-million-dollar job. The electricity for Times Square displays totals $15,000 a day, by one popular estimate. Con Edison, figuring that as of two years ago 360,000 forty-watt bulbs burned there, mails bills to over sixty persons or companies—though this spot may be the biggest user of power around 11 o'clock at night, there are many larger over-all consumers, such as Rockefeller Center. Admiral Television Appliances pays $1200 a month for juice. If all the elements of Canadian Club burned all the time, it would require over three quarters of a million watts, deliver over two and a half million candle power, and cost $6000 to $7000 a month. Space runs from $500 to $2500 a month, and many spectaculars rent annually for spectacular sums like $250,000. But what does money matter? Even the Salvation Army announces its presence with lights.

Times Square has a lot of low buildings, more than anywhere except in the city's outskirts, and many of them are dwarfed by the signs which soar from their squat roofs.

The TWA is four times as high as the two-story Toffenetti restaurant beneath it. Budweiser measures five stories. *Time-Life-Sports Illustrated* is nine stories, and Kleenex, eight. In the word Admiral, the A is 16 feet tall, the other letters, 11; Canadian Club letters are 12 to 22 feet; the capitals in TWA are 20 feet, or two stories. The B in Budweiser weighs over 3000 pounds.

Admiral, Pepsi, TWA, Kleenex, Canadian Club, and *Time-Life-Sports Illustrated* between them use 110,000 bulbs; five of the six require a total of ten miles of neon tubing; four of them have 550 miles of wiring.

All this display is mounted atop real estate which by itself wouldn't rate extra high at the tax bureau. Other intersections, like Wall Street and Broadway, or 42nd Street and Fifth Avenue, bring in more municipal revenue. If the rental in an average good area runs to $7 a square foot, in Times Square it might be only $4. The 35 parcels of land facing on the crossroads proper are assessed at $45,570,000, and the buildings at $14,415,000. For $59,985,000 you could in theory buy the whole place—the State of New York, however, sets valuations slightly higher, for a total of $65,917,500. The most valuable property is the Paramount, at $10,700,000; next comes the Astor Hotel, at $8,000,000; and they are the two buildings that carry no advertising other than identifying signs. The third building that most noticeably does without bright-lights income is, however, pretty well down on the assessors' list: the Times Tower.

Higher than most of its neighbors, and one of the pioneers, "The Times," in serene, delicately blue-white, unblinking English lettering presides with a supercilious air over the hurly-burly of the light-mad lower levels. Down at the dizzy crossroads itself, nobody has let that cramp his style. Mr. Peanut winks, Johnnie Walker with his 20-foot stride covers 44 miles a night. In what was called a "naturama," a streamlined train one-third actual size sped through the Grand Canyon. A funny little man danced for chewing gum on the Putnam Building. There were innocent, folksy subjects like Wrigley's playing fountains, the Eskimo Kids of Cliquot Club Ginger Ale, National Biscuit's Raincoat Boy, and the Corticelli kitten.

With a front foot valued at $1250, cash registers in drink spots and trinket shops can hardly ring up enough nickels and dimes to warrant the expensive location. Spectaculars pay the difference, and more. Sign makers erect the frames and usually leave them there, fitting to them the new materials required by changing customers. They can't spread out much farther. Except for the Astor, Times Tower, and Paramount, they have already pre-empted most of the space.

"A hundred Eiffel Towers, a thousand Rue Pigalle— luminous epilepsy, incandescent hypnotism"—a Frenchman thus rhapsodized about Times Square after World War I.

Others have said the lights dance, twinkle, rain, run, sparkle, circulate, flare, flow, writhe, roll, blink, wink, flicker, vanish, swirl, whirl, pour, dazzle, jump, leap, and shoot.

But while the Square outshines London even on Coronation Night, while the late producer William A. Brady might have hoped the last thing he looked on in this world would be the bright lights, while they have been applauded for a "barbaric magic that amounts to poetry," some men and women have objected. Practical criticism, on one hand, has been voiced by the fire department. A five-alarm blaze which in January 1959 broke out in the kitchen of a Howard Johnson restaurant and gutted four buildings at Broadway and 46th Street had a disastrous head start because, in theory, billboards solidly sheathed the walls and kept fighters from reaching the flames with axes and hose. New York Fire Commissioner Cavanagh warned that only a little more heat than was generated would have weakened the steel skeletons and brought them crashing into the street. He recommended laws to require openings in the surfaces of the signs.

But other critics complain on esthetic grounds. An Englishman lamented "cheapness and vulgarity everywhere." A native American forty years ago arraigned the electric signs which "with all their prodigal waste of light, are hideous to the eye and (they) insult the soul with base advertisements"; worse yet, he believed they betrayed the people's lack of any "defined artistic sense." "Generally speaking, the sign is the same nuisance in New York that it is in London or Paris—only more so," said another foreigner.

In 1896, the year after the Olympia opened, William Dean Howells denounced signs in general:

"If one thing in the business streets makes New York more hideous than another it is the signs, with their discordant colors, their infinite variety of tasteless shapes. If by chance there is any architectural beauty in a business edifice, it is spoiled, insulted, outraged by these huckstering appeals. . . . The darkness does not shield you from them. . . . The strangest part of all this is, no one finds it offensive, or at least no one says that it is offensive. . . . It seems as if the signs might eventually hide the city. That

105

would not be so bad if something could then be done to hide the signs."

Only late night can manage that. Around the corner along tinselly 42nd Street, the lights on the marquees, like midnight suns, hold fast to daytime till two or three or four in the morning. In the Square itself, dark settles in right after 12 o'clock. The Times Tower news lines black out, and those carried by CBS on the Bond Clothes building run only a few minutes longer.

Suddenly you miss a sound—the water in the Pepsi sign flows no more. The TWA plane's flashing signals cease, its propellers will not spin again till next day. Chevrolet leaves a gaping hole in the sky. Admiral is cut off. *Time-Life-Sports Illustrated* vanishes. The Scripto display stand ends its steady revolutions. Canadian Club quits, too. The Budweiser eagle flies away, and Johnnie Walker has had his constitutional.

The Playlands keep open, shooting the harsh bright shine of naked bulbs across the sidewalk. Howard Johnson serves his sweet-tooth customers till 4 o'clock. The narrow stairways to the dance halls, lined with photos of the frilly looking girls, lure the lonesome sailor. But the Square changes. Families have gone to bed. Grownups, mostly couples, stream through the intersection from the theaters. "Cross on the green," the sign warns, but traffic has thinned out and they cross in between. But they don't loiter for long. Midnight has struck, and one, and it is just another crossroads, with some litter blown into the corners, cold and muggy in winter, in summer warm and muggy and stale, all the glamour faded. Men lean against the wall, their rheumy eyes refusing to focus, or cling drunkenly to a post. Fellows in tight pants, their faces pimply and pale, slouch wearily down a subway entrance. They look like nighttime people, as if they never saw the day. A lone girl from the Astor hails a cab. There is loud and angry talk, and sometimes vulgar. The monotonous beat of jazz rises and subsides. But most surprising of all, there are silences.

The curtain has fallen, the show is over.

IX "If a table in Rector's could talk"

The first revolving door on Broadway began its dizzy existence the evening of September 23, 1899. Gentleman Jim Corbett and his wife made the first legitimate use of it, according to one story. According to another, it was a man we met at Koster and Bial's, George Kessler, Marietta de Dio's admirer. They came through this entrance for a business reason, that is to say, with money in their pockets. But the newfangled device for spinning indoors from out appealed to the uninvited public as such a novelty that several thousand people in a typical Times Square holiday mood had a whirl just for fun.

It admitted to the famous restaurant Rector's.

For a couple of tense hours of his hectic première, the dumfounded Charles Rector and his staff of sixty waiters, eight captains, and a score of bus boys watched the phenomenon of the biggest gate they could ever hope for matched nevertheless by receipts that didn't amount to a red penny. At last the paying customers, in stiff shirts, sweeping trains and cartwheel hats, fell into line and stayed for dinner.

The two-story yellow structure stood on the east side of

Broadway between 43rd and 44th Streets, the block below Hammerstein's Olympia. The second important building facing on the crossroads, it too pointed unmistakably toward the bright-lights, amusement district of the future. From the very start Times Square, while still called Longacre, was bent on being Times Square unconfined. During all its years, rural, genteel, de luxe, garish and frenetic, it was never wholly innocent of some Thieves'-Lair taint, either, for while it attracted irresistibly the man with a buck to squander, it also attracted with a sinister fatality the man with no scruples about how he made a buck. He, too, would dine in style at Rector's.

For a restaurateur who became the rage in this gay spot, Charles Rector possessed a surprisingly proper, sober air. But while the ends of his mustaches drooped solemnly, his son George's turned up in a debonair fashion, and thanks to his roly-poly cheeks and merry moist eye he could have acted Santa Claus with little make-up or modeling. George resembled the playboys who patronized the family establishment. Food, and also the horses, were weaknesses of his. He could scramble language pretentiously, but so could he sauces, and that won him the coveted Cordon Bleu after a real work-a-day apprenticeship in France at Marguery's and the Café de Paris.

George would remember this as the era of high-wheeled bicycles. They rolled by his windows and his novel door—he was the one to claim it was Broadway's first—going to and from the Michaux Bicycle Club upstreet, near the Brewster and Studebaker carriage plants from which the gasoline buggy soon would oust them all. Or he laboriously concocted a baroque phrase to describe the period: "When two bags of laundry and a Babylonian garden on the horizon would later prove to be a lady with leg-o'-mutton sleeves under a picture hat."

The crossroads, one hundred miles from Philadelphia's Rittenhouse Square, acquired the nickname "Eating-House Square." It was situated in the "Roaring Forties." The Knickerbocker bar with Maxfield Parrish's big mural of Old King Cole passed popularly as the "Forty-second Street Country Club." Across from it stood the Café de l'Opéra, generally pronounced de l'Oppra. Several thousand white-tie waiters bustling about here nightly with several thousand white napkins over their arms served 20,000 suppers including several thousand pounds of lobsters and several thousand bottles of champagne. Julian Street, the arbiter of elegance, christened it "Lobster Palace Society."

Maybe nowadays in Times Square yuh eat; in that golden age one dined.

The Knickerbocker two blocks south of Rector's possessed, for instance, a $10,000 gold service for catering to sixty persons. The hotel monogram decorated tablecloths, napkins, and doilies, all of the same pattern. Almost worth its weight in gold, the china for private parties consisted of "bleue de Sèvres," a title that merits quotation marks. Manufactured to order, all the blue and gold dishes in the 72-piece set bore the monogram on the rim. Chicken browned tastily nested in a solid silver casserole, and fruit in a silver wickerwork basket.

Rector's rivaled the Knickerbocker in everything but size. There Diamond Jim Brady dazzled the public with his acres of diamonds, maintaining that those that has 'em wears 'em. Tucking a napkin 28 inches square in around his collar, this bedizened trencherman sat down to gargantuan feasts of so many oysters, lobsters, chops, steaks and other dishes that George Rector saluted him as "the best 25 customers we had." Within a year of the purchase of $30,000 worth of table linen in Belfast, Rector had to replace a third of it because of thefts, burns from cigars, wine stains and the dollar sign and figures scrawled over its glossy surface by customers dreaming of profits or scared of losses. Some 2000 pieces of silver vanished annually at a cost of $20,000. One woman tried to snitch a percolator; worth only $75, it scorched her $7500 furs.

Like the linen, all the silver carried the stiff-backed Rector griffin, a creature with devil's tail, lion's body, eagle's head and wings, and Scotch collie ears. Its original habitat was the Frontier House in Lewiston, New York, on the Niagara River, where in 1825 the founder of the Rector line was owner, cook, and bottlewasher at the Sign of the Griffin. He dispensed plain, substantial, good food, like ham and eggs—which the snobbish New York Rector's never served without glorifying it as *jambon* and *oeufs*. The successful proprietor moved to Rockport on the Erie Canal to open a hotel.

Two sons enlisted in the Civil War. Charles, the lone survivor, got a job in New York, which inauspiciously cold-shouldered him that time: he was conductor on a Second Avenue horsecar. Transferring ambitiously to Chicago to work for George Pullman, he managed the first Pullman Hotel Dining Car to cross the continent. But the restaurateur dormant in him gnawed away, he hankered for his own business, and finally hoisted the griffin at Rector's Oyster House at Clark and Monroe Streets. A grand staircase led down into his dining room so that a lady could spread her train wide for a queenly entrance. To attract a distinguished clientele he imported unfamiliar delicacies. Chicagoans had sampled oysters and lobsters pickled, smoked, or preserved in some style, but he brought them back alive, and with them a green turtle the size of a raft for soup. He introduced still another novelty: one of the first cash registers to ring a bell that far west.

For the World's Fair of 1893, the city issued only one restaurant license, his son would recall, and it was for Rector's Café Marine. Visiting firemen patronized it—Brady again, George M. Cohan, Stanford White, Richard Harding Davis, Lillian Russell. They all supplied invaluable testimonials when, urged on by Kessler, he decided to try his luck in New York. The helpful Kessler even picked a location. Jack Dunston and Thomas Healy couldn't finance the Broadway building erected for them—though Dunston would found his own famous Jack's on Sixth Avenue. Rector moved in behind the showy Greco-Roman façade intended for them and spotlighted his griffin above his entrance; the wandering bird-beast would roost at one more home before, almost one hundred years old, it passed away. The new owner set up 100 tables on the first floor and 75 on the second, and prepared four private dining rooms. A Russian string orchestra played, mostly George M. Cohan. Mirrors glittered from floor to ceiling, and clients trod on thick red carpeting amid trimmings green and gold, Louis XIV and Byzantine. Total bill for floss and plush amounted to $200,000; and rent, $10,000 a year.

The international bill of fare listed Egyptian quail, Scotch woodcock, English pheasant, African peaches. An eccentric ate backward, from nuts to soup. Still another dined there two years on a diet exclusively of snails and champagne, and then died, though perhaps without this

encouragement an illness already contracted would have carried him off then anyway. A contemporary writer charged stuffily that "nobody of distinction of appetite goes to a lobster palace to eat." But he was wrong. Besides gourmands like Diamond Jim Brady among its patrons, it catered to gourmets. Sarah Bernhardt enjoyed one of her favorite dishes there, canapé of crab meat Rector. Sir Thomas Lipton graced the private table for yachtsmen, among them Commodore Cornelius Vanderbilt. The chef won the special transatlantic commendation of Queen Victoria—or wouldn't that indicate superior food?

For his army of waiters, the meticulous Rector prescribed a uniform of full evening dress with divided coattails and white vests; he forbade beards, mustaches, glasses and dickeys, or detachable shirt fronts—though about every cook in his kitchens could boast of a flourishing mustache that reached out as far as his ears. But munificent earnings compensated agreeably for the strict regulations. The maître d'hôtel, on top of a regular $150 a month, got Christmas and New Year's tips which totaled $20,000 or $30,000, or so Rector supposed. To his $25 from the boss, a waiter added $800 or more a month handed out by the prodigal customers. Part of his income depended on his knack for inducing the public to drink champagne; salesmen for various companies, like Kessler of Moët et Chandon, slipped him premiums of 25 cents for the cork of a sparkling pint and 50 cents for the quart size. At the start an employee on a wage basis presided over the check room; when he offered Rector $100 a month for his job and all the perquisites, the naïve proprietor signed him on. Learning better before long, Rector himself collected $10,000 a year for this, while the prosperous concessionaire engaged his own Wall Street broker to invest his windfall.

George claimed later that, with all meals à la carte, people could eat well for $1.25. But most of the customers fared better than well, since he also listed the average dinner check at $2; his New Year's Eve take at $10,000; Saturday nights, $5000; ordinary nights, $2000. Estimates vary, however. According to Julian Street, a choice supper with champagne for two could set a gentleman back $12 or $14, plus $2 or $3 tips to waiter and head waiter at the nearby and comparable Café de l'Opéra, the blue-and-gold night spot with napery glowing pink above the underlighted tabletops, and with black marble columns and black marble staircase at the foot of which stood the cousin of Rector's griffin: a winged lion having a man's head.

If we compare Rector's to our "21," we identify a predecessor of Sardi's in Shanley's where fifty years ago a menu offered sirloin steak, minute steak, tournedos of beef or brook trout, $1.50; roast turkey, $1.40; squab, $1; two lamb chops, 70 cents.

In those days the bars spread a free lunch out on their open counters. And mighty lucky at that, cried one bankrupt diner who pretended that anyone footing a bill at Rector's would need free lunches for a month to catch up. Even so, the dollar used to go farther. Joe Laurie, Jr., has written nostalgically, "You could almost have given a party at Rector's, Churchill's, or Shanley's for what a tab for two at the Stork Club, Twenty-One, the Colony, or Chambord comes to!"

All around the Square the lobster palaces and restaurants bowed and scraped year in and year out to much the same roster of permanent guests: Stanford White, Evelyn

Nesbit Thaw, Lew Dockstader, Richard Canfield, Oscar Hammerstein I, George Kessler, George M. Cohan, O. Henry, Stephen Crane, Clyde Fitch, Richard Harding Davis, Rex Beach, Victor Herbert, Nat Goodwin and one or another of the Mrs. Goodwins. Rector remembered three husband-and-wife couples spinning in through his revolving door for a gay party together; every one of the men had once been married to every one of the women. Wilson Mizner, returning after a trip, surveyed the crowd in Rector's and gibed: "Same old faces. But they're paired off differently."

Victor Herbert, hearing an orchestra in Shanley's perform music of his on which it paid no royalty, indignantly filed suit and collected. This legal victory prompted the formation of the American Society of Composers, Authors and Performers, or ASCAP, according to one legend. That may not be true. There is no doubt, however, about a second story told by Rector: Cohan while living at Rector's Hotel wrote many songs, among them "Mary Is a Grand Old Name," "Yankee Doodle Dandy," and "Give My Regards to Broadway."

Cohan drumming his piano in his suite was not the only man to transact business in Times Square resorts. At the grill of the Claridge, successor to Rector's, and at the Knickerbocker grill, and in the Astor's public rooms, Cecil B. De Mille, Jesse L. Lasky, Sam Goldwyn, Adolph Zukor, Zukor's son Eugene, Mary Pickford, John Barrymore, and others made the deals that shaped the movie industry. It was to the Victoria Theater at 42nd Street and Seventh Avenue that Arthur Hammerstein hurried to gloat with his brother Willie, the manager there, over Otto H. Kahn's $100,000 check. That constituted an installment on the sum

118

that would buy father Oscar's second Manhattan Opera House and along with it his promise to stay out of opera. The two boys, who in despair had watched parental fortunes poured down the music drain, crossed back over Seventh, Broadway and 42nd to the Knickerbocker to celebrate with champagne. Today it could not be the Knickerbocker, which until recently housed *Newsweek* magazine, and cocktails or highballs would substitute for Kessler's favorite vintage.

Though Rector's had less dining space than some of its neighbors, it catered to the elite with no less success. It tempted in particular the late revellers, and along with them, Broadway celebrities, musical comedy stars, "name" actors, actresses, and show girls. Reginald Vanderbilt, Alfred Gwynne Vanderbilt, John Jacob Astor, and Jesse Lewisohn entertained in its private rooms. Society retired secretively behind its doors for cards, and often hiked the kitty up to $1200. The Partridge Club met there, with poker at a $20 limit; to vary their fun, they sat for table stakes, with a pot that could zoom off wildly to $20,000 or $30,000. The chauffeurs parked their upright, carriagelike, black automobiles in the Square among the vanishing hacks, or at some garage where, in a snug room reserved for them, they removed their dusters and visored caps, hung up their goggles and played games themselves till their masters summoned them.

George Rector boasted, "I found Broadway a quiet little lane of ham and eggs in 1899, and I left it a full-blown avenue of lobsters, champagne, and morning-afters." He and his father cleared $1,000,000. George married a girl Charles didn't like. Charles decided alone to add a hotel to his property. They quarreled and separated, they patched

it up, and then they encountered real trouble, with dramatist Paul Potter unintentionally to blame. Adapting a
French farce to Broadway, he needed a title; the sight of
a girl stepping out of a hansom and entering Rector's one
rainy day suggested, *The Girl from Rector's*. It was pre-
mièred at Weber's Theater February 1, 1909, and Rector
senior claimed it ruined him. Evidently it did, but it's
harder to understand why the insipid work didn't ruin au-
thor Potter, too.

At the rise of the curtain, a doorbell rang, and the first
spoken words were:

"Who's agitating the tinkler?"

Anyone who stayed on after this inanity—and everybody did, for the play was popular—heard more of the
same, for instance a pun: in response to a reference to "the
Rector's girl," there came the question "Which rector?"

It might be assumed that this fatuous dialogue would
drive everybody away not only from the theater but from
the smart restaurant at this sophisticated crossroads. But
something else antagonized the public. The "Rector's girl,"
Loute Sedaine, posed back home as the ultrarespectable
Mrs. Grimes Caperton, but in New York she lived in sin
with Richard Van Arsdale. With the end of his infatuation
and his wholesome decision to marry sweet, pure Marcia,
thus redeeming himself if not Rector's or Times Square,
he explained:

"I drop the Night Owl Club, Rector's, Jack's, Churchill's,
the Gay Girls, the Hangers On, the illicit joys of little old
New York."

Of that one speech Potter could have been proud, for the
straightforward, unfancy statement was social history: in
effect Richard abandoned Times Square.

But patrons fell away from Rector's in hordes not because the conversation sounded witless but because a man installed his mistress there, not because Rector's wasn't fun but because it was. Naughty Loute destroyed it. No husband dared write his wife from that wicked address. For three months after George and his father together opened their remodeled establishment in 1911, the dining room had few guests to serve, and losses amounted, like the wages of sin, to $1000 a day. George M. Cohan rescued his friends from this fix, at least temporarily. Still retaining his lease in the Hotel Knickerbocker, he generously rented an extra suite of five rooms at Rector's, moved in his piano and publicly professed himself a patron once more. For a while business rushed back. But all the months of the year were beginning disastrously to resemble slow and profitless August when Saratoga lured away the moneyed folks. The hotel closed, the father retired. George experimented with a less exclusive place at Broadway and 48th Street, offered entertainment and would declare afterward, "It was Rector's that introduced dancing with meals." What Paul Potter supposedly did for the hotel, however, prohibition did with absolute finality for the second restaurant, and George sold out. On January 1, 1919, he hauled down the griffin forever.

"If a table in Rector's could talk," as Nat Wills sang in the first *Ziegfeld Follies,* it would talk about romance, naturally, but also out of firsthand observation about social glamour and verve half a century ago.

New Yorkers dressed better, or more New Yorkers dressed, in that decade or two than at any other time in one hundred years. The head waiter would admit to the Café de l'Opéra, though not exactly welcome, a guest without white shirt front, but he would shunt him upstairs. But in the 1860s, as Daniel Frohman remembered, with Washington Square the residential center and Delmonico's moved way uptown, as they viewed it, to Fifth Avenue and 14th Street, people stepped out for a fashionable evening without evening clothes. Frohman wrote:

"When a man wanted to go to the theater, he would usually meet his wife downtown because the horsecars were slow and there would not be time to go home and come back again to the theater. Full dress was not *de rigueur* because horsecars and bus traffic were the most popular form of transportation, except among the wealthy who could hire a private coach."

Ladies were all laundry bags and Babylonian gardens: hats to obliterate the view of a stage, concocted out of osprey feathers, ostrich plumes, flowers, laces, and hatpins with swollen jeweled knobs; and pinched waists that squeezed out balloon effects above and below. Gentlemen's high stiff collars sawed at their jowls, and they wore diamond stickpins. For afternoon they appeared in pearl derby, white vest, and cutaway coat with buttonhole nosegay. One Beau Brummel reportedly sewed lapels on his underwear.

It is to the simpler years antedating the lobster palace that today's informal, democratic fashions revert. The manager of a Times Square hotel with which he has been associated almost half a century recalls forlornly:

"Every one of my clerks once wore evening dress at the desk. Now if some one comes along Broadway in a tux, you look to see if his front is going to light up and he's trying to sell you a cigar.

"Around World War I if anybody went out Saturday

night he dressed, at least in this neighborhood. Martin's at Broadway and 41st Street admitted nobody without dinner clothes. Then you could pick the fish that was swimming, now if you pick one lobster they give you another."

In his lobby with its splendid hammered bronze chandeliers almost two generations old, with carved pilasters and polished marble paneling, the guests now are boys in bright-figured sports shirts and no ties, tourists in sweaters and canvas-toed shoes, girls with pony tails puffing cigarettes. They have money, but they don't waste it on style. It reminded the manager:

"You used to be able to tell a prostitute by the fact that she let you see her smoking."

Then, not forgetting his olden-day manners in his modern inn, he begged, "Excuse me, sir," and walked off to retrieve from a green embossed jardiniere and deposit properly in an ash tray a wet, red-stained butt flipped there by a blonde in slacks.

Rector's has been transformed into one restaurant in a chain of spick-and-span chromium places with an open serving counter right in the dining room where clients resting their elbows on hard-topped uncovered tables can see for themselves how hygienic it is. But in all the Square, the Astor Hotel, where Medcef Eden had his farmhouse, comes closest to maintaining its plush, starchy status. It still feeds 5000 at one sitting, and caters to presidents, ambassadors, and generals. W. C. Fields used to bat a handball around in his suite there. Charles Evans Hughes slept there the one night he believed the country had elected him to the White House. Novelist James Michener stops there, explaining, "When I'm in New York, I want to be in the middle of it." Jimmy Durante, Arturo Toscanini, Omar

Bradley, Jack Dempsey, Lee and J. J. Shubert, John Drew, William Gillette, John Golden, Will Rogers, Douglas Mac-Arthur, and every President since Theodore Roosevelt—today and yesterday they preferred the Astor.

Lots of West Pointers—the Navy patronized Jack's and Shanley's—have chosen the Astor as New York headquarters and loitered in the bar—they still do. In emergencies they used to touch William Muschenheim, former West Point steward who built the place and presided over it for years, for enough money to get back upriver. The present manager is a tall, handsome, full-blooded prince, the Russian-born Serge Obolensky. Even with his noble heritage, he can't revive the spade-whisker, stock-collar, pince-nez, Prince Albert era.

Once upon a time the ladies looped a long, elegant train over a lovely bare arm to promenade in the spacious lobby; ambassadors pinned on jeweled medals and drew bright-colored sashes at an angle down across their immaculate shirt fronts. The chair backs were ornately patterned, the walls gorgeously tapestried. A circular so old that more horses than autos appear in the picture of the street outside appealed to potential guests: "Imagine a ballroom, the largest of five great halls, the size of an opera house; gorgeous in decoration, with a gilded lattice canopy of solid bronze through which light filters down in soft radiance, or falls in cataracts of splendor, as occasion demands; fitted with a disappearing stage (and) the largest organ in the world"—no jazz band yet. There were mahogany doors and wainscoting; Royal Spanish Renaissance parlors; a Flemish bar with a painting of "Long Acre Farm" by the popular E. G. Unitt, who among other public activities designed the scenery for Daniel Frohman at the Lyceum, and at

Daly's; a Louis XIV dining room; and two *art nouveau* rooms which now in pictures look anything but *art* or *nouveau*.

While the Astor maintained its tone, the Square around it began to slip. It grew boisterous, tough, and rowdy. For major celebrations, especially after elections, fearful of the crowds and crush in the streets, Rector's boarded up the windows and admitted by card only. Those occasions proved noisier even than New Year's when George helped jockey Tod Sloan, Julia Sanderson's husband, to hoist his small brass cannon up the two stories to the roof and bang away in competition with the *Times'* fireworks. But it wasn't always fun. A drunken collegian made the mistake of tackling Fred Stone, the Scarecrow of *The Wizard of Oz* in person and a matinee idol, as everyone knew, and also, as fewer people knew, an amateur boxer; when the boy tried to block him in the revolving door, Stone knocked him out cold. Kessler, whom we've seen in a pommeling match with Hammerstein, tangled with a friend at his table. In a joshing mood, each reached across to give the other's tie a yank; Kessler played rough, his angry companion grabbed nastily for his ear, and up flew their fists.

But George Rector was right, the wilder night spots lay around a corner. At Jack's, some one itching for trouble would lob a saltcellar or champagne glass across the room. In smaller restaurants loud-mouthed, scrappy revellers escorted overdressed young women. A drunk passed out on the floor and his gay partner flipped up her skirts to jump over him before he was carried out. A girl came alone, and could be sure of a gentleman to take her home. Some lobster palaces induced frankly a relaxed attitude between the sexes. They didn't decorate with murals of Old King Cole—

who today holds sway in the Hotel St. Regis; Julian Street pretended he was surprised to find the good king instead of the king's harem at the Knickerbocker. Walls in flashy bars pictured a Babylon where near nudes stalked boldly.

Something faded, or withered, or soured. You could see it in the crowds, the window displays, even in the restaurants. A composer used to jot down tunes on the starched linen which dragged its four corners on Shanley's floor; a movie magnate figured his income on it. Nowadays a composer or financier would have a good long hunt through Times Square for a place with a regular old-fashioned tablecloth. When the gambler Herman Rosenthal was murdered in front of Considine's Metropole, a friendly waiter brought out a tablecloth as big as a sheet to spread over the body. To cover a corpse today, most of the eateries could provide only plastic mats and paper napkins.

X "You're smart Jew boys"

A man might as well commit murder in Macy's window as in Times Square. How could he hope to escape? Dozens of traffic officers are on duty there, and brawny cops in unbeatable pairs patrol some streets around the clock. Besides, a killing could have a thousand eyewitnesses.

An occasional criminal might delude himself with the notion that this faceless multitude promised safety. But when, abandoning caution, he does his shooting in Times Square, his victim draws down on him headlines as big and black as doom.

It almost happened at Rector's. At least the proprietor recalled—but he was no man to kill a story just because it wasn't true—that a gambler who had dined there with his girl was slain by her right after they left in a cab. The cabbies themselves had dubious reputations. Among them were Gas-House Sam, Ten-Cent Dan, Mississippi, Bounding Dick, Tenderloin Bill, Frank the Gyp; did one of them drive for Rector's ill-fated couple? They sound like the names of the quartet that ambushed Rosenthal. They could steer a drunken fare through Central Park and stick him up in the dark. Reputable doormen tried to forestall these holdups if only because they knew slicker ways of separating a sucker from his roll and wanted the first whack at it themselves.

But Rector remembered a nearer, more harrowing miss in 1906. Stanford White dined there frequently. Arriving in evening dress, and alone, for his very last visit, he chose a table close to the entrance so that he could see and be seen by other guests. A nervous, pale young man burst in, George Rector stepped up to greet him and help him off with his coat. It caught on a pistol butt in his hip pocket. The newcomer cast a quick look around, spotted White, turned even paler, threw his coat back on, and ducked out faster than he came in. A few nights later this nerve-wracked customer, Harry K. Thaw, tracked White down in Madison Square Garden and shot him. The sequel was enacted back in Times Square some years later in 1913. The glamorous Evelyn Nesbit Thaw, who stirred up the hot blood, was booked by Willie Hammerstein into the Victoria. One of vaudeville's biggest drawing cards, she earned $3500 a week for eight weeks, while the happy box office's harvest grew to $80,000. She opened, it happened, just the week of Thaw's escape from Matteawan.

But Times Square's chief criminals, the pair really in earnest about it, were Herman Rosenthal and Arnold Rothstein.

"You're smart Jew boys," Big Tim Sullivan told them when they were mere apprentice gamblers.

State senator and Tammany boss, Big Tim calculated that he could levy on the games these two might some day run for the stuss, poker and dice kingdom which he ruled. But Rosenthal, far from smart, was such a blabbermouth and whiner that few people would mourn his death;

and while a biographer granted Rothstein "the smartest unsocial mind of his time," he was to suffer the same ultimate agony as Rosenthal.

These pernicious characters were guilty of no crime of passion, except, of course, the gambling passion, the heartless passion. They battled for underworld control. Tribute money from houses of prostitution bulked large in the take, but no torrid Evelyn Nesbit Thaw or seductive Loute Sedaine diverted them from more baleful designs. The advertising line on a paperback cover read, "A tough private eye mixes dames and death in Times Square." That held true for fiction only. The recent knifing in Birdland, almost within arm's reach of a 15-piece ear-splitting jazz band madly sending one hundred addicts, evidently had no sex angle to redeem it; neither did the murder of Albert Anastasia in the barbershop of the very hotel to which another slayer treacherously summoned Rothstein.

The careers of Herman Rosenthal and Arnold Rothstein, the ugliest in the history of craps and cards, and of Times Square, too, were climaxed in duplicate violence and bloodshed. Launched right at the crossroads itself, they whirled around it in a vicious circle, and wound up within easy pistol shot of the starting point.

The drab property room of the Victoria Theater spawned this couple. Willie Hammerstein's stagehands whiled away their extra idle hours Monday afternoons by rolling dice. First some harmless sports happened to wander in off Broadway; next came tougher characters, some members of the Hudson Duster gang from the old Tenderloin, for example, and Gophers. Though Willie's friends credited him with wanting religiously to stop the gambling, it was never curbed as long as the building stood.

Furthermore, it turned from playful to deadly serious. A few boys would achieve phenomenal entries in police annals, among them Monk Eastman, Whitey Lewis, and Dago Frank. But the pick of this band passed under the notorious names of Rosenthal and Rothstein.

Rosenthal, a bit corpulent, of medium height and brunet coloring, had a face flat as a board, a high empty forehead, and lips that curled for a facile sneer. The night he reported artlessly for the rendezvous with his killers at the Metropole, owned by Big Tim in association with the Considine brothers, he wore a dark suit, and his brass belt buckle was stamped with the initials HR.

Beansy, as they called Rosenthal, labored under the dismal reputation of being a petty gambler from downtown who kidded himself into thinking he deserved a cut in the lush uptown racket, but who lacked the brains to swing it. A crap game that paid off lost money under his bungling direction; he couldn't, for instance, break even with the Hesper Club, though Big Tim's brother Paddy cleaned up on it.

His fatal mistake occurred in refusing to play along with Police Lieutenant Charles S. Becker; and conversely, Becker's fatal mistake, as he would learn, occurred in trying to compel him to. Becker, whose jutting lower lip and heavily lidded eyes gave him a simian look, had evolved in twenty years into an arrogant and ruthless cop determined to latch onto gangland power. He was smarter than Rosenthal, which isn't saying much; but he wasn't smart enough, either. He shot a boy, as one official boner; and as another, jailed an innocent woman. Credited with rescuing a man from drowning in the East River, he became a hero; but the suspicion that the whole business was a plant cut him down

ignominiously to a fourflusher. On a salary of $138 a week, he saved $70,000.

When Big Tim Sullivan fell ill, Lieutenant Becker conspired to usurp the underworld kingship. Hiring Big Jack Zelig as strong-arm man, he sent him out on the regular rounds to collect the tribute. But to Big Jack's demand, Beansy Rosenthal offered a mulish defiance: he would fork over his percentage to Big Tim as usual, and no one else. Though Zelig tried to build up Becker as the new boss, he just didn't know enough one-syllable words to be able to explain to Rosenthal. Yet something penetrated that dim wit, for he took the precaution of setting up as his body-guard the plug-ugly pair of Bridgie Webber and Sam Paul. Zelig reacted fast: his gang smashed Paul's gambling joint to pieces and inflicted a savage beating on him. Even a moron could interpret this violence, and Rosenthal grudgingly did as he was told: accepted Becker as hidden partner in his Hesper Club.

Instead of resigning himself to Becker's dominance, instead of knuckling under and staying knuckled, he had to whine. Becker peremptorily ordered him to be quiet, but he wouldn't, or in sober truth couldn't; his perverse nature would oblige him to snivel and whimper himself into the Metropole doorway and the arms of his killers. That settled it for Becker, who promptly staged a raid on the Hesper Club exactly as though he didn't own a piece of it. Some time later when the rebellious Rosenthal, who must have lost his mind, refused to ante up for the defense fund of a Becker aide accused of murder, Rosenthal himself one night walked head-on into a wicked clobbering.

With incredible stupidity he felt confident he could buck the powerful lieutenant. He promised newsman Herbert

Bayard Swope to talk for the *World,* and spread the rumor that he had, intending to scare Becker. Becker wasn't scaring. Infuriated by this challenge, he wasn't waiting any longer, either. He gave Zelig $2000 blood money. Zelig conscripted four killers hard to match in the history of crime: Gyp the Blood, a cutthroat bouncer whose real name was Harry Horowitz; Lefty Louie, or Louis Rosenberg, pickpocket and pimp; Dago Frank, or Francesco Cirofici, dope addict; and Whitey Lewis, or Jacob Seidenshiner, one-time prize fighter handy with a blackjack.

These four stalked like executioners into the Garden Café on Seventh Avenue, and marched in a beeline to Rosenthal's table. Two stuck their hands out with guns cupped forebodingly in them, and Beansy Rosenthal's heart must have skipped so many beats they might as well have shot him then and there. That night his gambler's luck held: he was treating his wife to dinner, and the elemental underworld code included a rule not to mess a man up in the presence of his family.

But this diabolical apparition panicked him. He decided to tell Swope, figuring he could pin charges on Becker exclusively, omitting the others, and get away with it. He spilled all his damning facts about the links between police and dice and card games. Swope printed every word, and scored a sensational scoop.

Beansy didn't believe the writing on the wall, or probably couldn't read it. He didn't believe Big Tim who had protected him was on the skids; didn't believe Rothstein who told him he must beat it out of town to save his neck and offered him the money for it; didn't believe a "Policeman Baker" who, his wife would report, warned him to flee for his life; didn't believe an anonymous red-ink note: "You will never live to testify against the police." With any brains at all, he would have realized the meaning of these repeated threats: time was running out.

District Attorney Charles S. Whitman summoned him but he absolutely would not talk. Then on the fatal Monday, seized by terror and despair, he changed his mind. He begged Rothstein for the cash already offered and refused, but Rothstein pronounced sentence: too late. He hurried to Whitman and exposed all. A telephone call invited him to the Metropole a step east of Broadway.

What could happen right in Times Square?

Beansy arrived before midnight. Many diners whom he passed on the way to his table were acquainted with him, but turned away ominously and took care to show no sign of recognition. Maybe they attended Sam Paul's outing the day before at Northport, where the picnickers made no bones about predicting that if Herman Rosenthal didn't shut his mouth he would die.

After about two hours, some one, perhaps a waiter, delivered a message in a voice which carried to patrons nearby:

"Herman, some one wants you outside."

Four men waited there. One spoke:

"Here, Beansy."

Then they jumped him and fired.

It blended like one shot, according to the lead story that very morning in the *Times*, so close that the city desk might have heard the guns. Bullets splattered into Beansy's face. His hands clawed at the wounds. He slumped to the walk. One killer heaved him over so he could check the pulse. Then he raced across the street to his companions already

135

piling into the getaway car. The lumbering auto with high straight sides roared off.

A doctor from a neighboring office examined the body. The surgeon in the Flower Hospital ambulance declared officially: dead. A Metropole waiter decently spread a tablecloth over the disfigured remains. A man who pretended he had dashed up from an innocent drink of soda at a fountain in Cohan's Theater building leaned over the victim, shook him as if to arouse him, and demanded:

"Who did it, Herman?"

That the law waited two long weeks to answer was perhaps not so surprising as pious folks complained. Reformer Parkhurst had forced his revelations on an uninterested, complacent city twenty years before. State Senator Lexow had come and investigated and gone, and the public conscience, a lazy organ at best, had fallen contentedly out of the habit of worrying about grafting officers. Even the *Times*, though it felt a special responsibility since the crossroads which borrowed its spotless name had degenerated into Rosenthal's hangout, originally was disposed to make light of Whitman's effort to implicate the police. This should have been an avoidable astigmatism, because its own first story, if read correctly, contained a clue to justify this investigator's course: Herman Rosenthal only a few days before, it commented, had defied Lieutenant Becker by locking up the cop Becker assigned to guard his premises after the raid. Republican Whitman, with the square jaw and the stiff straw hat, knew what he was doing, and had the luck, the will or the something to sail into the governorship of New York on it in 1914.

Maybe the abundance of lurid columns provided by the busy daily papers helped the two weeks to pass tolerably fast. Six slayers rode off in a white car, said the *Times,* but changed to four slayers and a gray car. Cops had appeared almost instantaneously—naturally, the cynical public charged, posted purposely so no one would hinder Zelig's killers; and two bystanders would remember that shortly before the hour of the murder they had been ordered not to loiter in front of the Metropole. But that did an injustice to some officers. In the restaurant in civilian clothes when the shots rang out, one sprinted to the street, bowling over a waiter in his haste, and saw the auto speed toward Sixth Avenue, and would have fired but for the many people who sprang out of nowhere between him and his target. Two others joined him and commandeered a taxi stationed next door at the Cadillac Hotel; wasting invaluable seconds in a U-turn, it lost the criminals. Still another policeman kept the gathering crowd at a distance.

Day by day more witnesses were rounded up. A barber and his wife alerted by the hubbub had spotted Bridgie Webber. An actor and a clerk at the Elks Club on 43rd Street near Sixth Avenue were able to describe the fugitives as young. The abandoned car, a key item in the investigation, was recovered before dawn. Louis Libby, the owner, earned a living by renting it. Arrested on a homicide count, he identified as his driver William Shapiro, who had reported, he admitted, "a little shooting." Shapiro claimed he had pretended to stall when the four thugs jumped in to escape, but they assured him it was safe and they had plenty of reason to believe what they told him:

"The police are fixed."

The license plate, which the Elks clerk glimpsed, contained fatefully two 13s: 41313. A woman's quick eye caught the double 13—the 4 was hidden from her—on a machine parked the night of the crime in front of Becker's house at 165th Street and Edgecombe Avenue. The net pulled tighter with the revelation that Becker's friend Big Jack Zelig did business with Libby.

Becker's movements were probed by Whitman, who got no help from New York's Mayor William J. Gaynor or his police commissioner, at least at the start. The district attorney employed the William J. Burns Detective Agency. How did the lieutenant with murder on his mind spend the evening? He watched boxing at Madison Square Garden; and the cold-blooded Becker could no doubt forget the death he had ordained for Rosenthal while he exulted over a gory main bout ended by the refusal of Dave Kurtz of Newark to leave his corner to suffer any more of a beating from Buck Crouse of Pittsburgh. After stopping in Park Row for the early papers, Becker drove uptown. He went through 42nd Street and swung brazenly up Broadway right around the corner from the slaying and not many minutes before it. Riding with him was Jack Sullivan, the man who drank the soda and, just as if he didn't know, asked Herman who did it.

Soon after he reached home, a henchman, Jack Rose, hurried to the *Times'* Broadway entrance; picked at random a pay telephone, and not inside a booth, either, as if it didn't matter whether anyone overheard; and told the boss his good news: Beansy would never squeal again—Becker would claim that only a newsman phoned. Billiard Ball Jack Rose, reported to be New York's best poker player, called for Libby's car and Shapiro that night. Jack Rose had wangled out of Dora Gilbert, Rosenthal's first wife, an affidavit against him in case Becker needed it. Jack Rose on his way to the scene of the crime picked up a man at 42nd Street and Sixth, portentously near Bridgie Webber's joint. Jack Rose was identified by the vindictive Rosenthal as Becker's go-between and collector who handled the mortgage money which proved Becker had a finger in the Hesper Club.

Though officials felt, or pretended to feel, considerable doubt about Becker's guilt—hadn't he sent Rosenthal's stricken widow $50 for funeral expenses?—they played it safe and made the gesture of transferring him to a desk job and assigning him to an outlying borough station. His jaunty, insolent air stuck defiantly with him until just two weeks from the day of the shooting, when Whitman indicted him for murder. This followed the arrests of Sam Paul, Bridgie Webber, Jack Sullivan, Harry Vallon who was Jack Rose's passenger, and Dago Frank, nabbed in a Harlem flat drugged with opium. James Verella, café proprietor, provided this tip-off at the cost of his life, and Big Jack Zelig also was slain before he could testify.

Dago Frank and his fellow gunmen Gyp the Blood, Lefty Louie and Whitey Lewis burned in the electric chair in April 1914, but Becker staved off retribution longer. The accusation that he was framed to cover up for Big Tim Sullivan never gained much credence, and he didn't talk. He died in Sing Sing the night of July 30, 1915. Arnold Rothstein and some friends sat ghoulishly around a table at Jack's to wait for his end at eleven o'clock.

That raised the curtain on Rothstein, who didn't go to the chair and perhaps didn't deserve it, and was not convicted of any crime though he often deserved it. He died with his shoes on, however; and his murder exactly like Rosenthal's was investigated in only a perfunctory and indifferent manner by the police—without benefit of a Whitman.

He traveled a crooked road from a respectable Jewish home and a decent orthodox family life, from his birth in 1882 due east of Times Square on 47th Street to Lindy's Restaurant and the Park Central Hotel. The public had heard little about him, beyond incidental mention in connection with Rosenthal. After his precocious initiation at Hammerstein's into the perilous world of cards and dice for keeps, he branched out on his own by renting a barn to entertain gamblers, and set himself up as proprietor of a minor dive in a West 45th Street basement. In 1909 he married beautiful Carolyn Greene, an actress.

He had the reputation of the deadly cool gambler alert for the kill, and the big kill, too, with lightning-fast fingers to manipulate the marked deck and rake in the cash and chits. He had lightning-fast foot action, too. Five gunmen raided a crap game of his in a West 47th Street hotel room just after the wily Rothstein had collected a fat wad of bills. He dropped it and kicked it under the edge of the rug to save it. Suspecting one player in the party had tipped off the visitors, he glued his eyes on him till the holdup gang left so he couldn't signal the hiding place to them.

Once in a Harlem game he was robbed of $28,000. In a single year bets on two races netted him $1,350,000. Blamed for fixing the 1919 World Series, he seems for a change innocent, an onlooker but no more. Prodigiously versatile and adaptable, he acted supposedly as receiver in a $5,000,000 bond theft; he arrogantly assigned himself lead roles in labor racketeering, dope traffic, and bootlegging. With several captivating steerers, he dragged in the wealthy for a fleecing at cards or dice in the genteel surroundings of the Café de l'Opéra, the Metropole, Jack's or Shanley's, where it shouldn't have hurt so much.

Beginning the evening of September 8, 1928, and running on disastrously to the morning of September 10, Rothstein played his final major poker game in Jimmy Meehan's apartment at 54th Street and Seventh Avenue. With George McManus serving technically as host, the guests included some hard-boiled out-of-town gamblers. For once Rothstein had a pressing use for money, if only because he and Carolyn were drawing up a divorce settlement. Yet for once he behaved like a simpleton. He borrowed heavily, and ran up debts wildly. With the last hand called and the last card turned up, he owed one man $219,000, another $73,000, and a third $30,000. Except for his word, he left them absolutely nothing to show for it, because as soon as he figured out each ruinous total and announced it, he tore up his IOUs.

The underworld code fixed the responsibility on McManus, who assured his leery company Rothstein would make good. But a wait that lengthened to a week set McManus to sweating. Rothstein branded the game crooked, and wondered aloud why he should pay at all, McManus heard. Rumor indicated he might welsh. On a spot and scared to death, McManus offered a confederate ten per cent to collect. He had the nerve to accost Rothstein right on Broadway and threaten him. Rothstein answered in a savage temper.

On Sunday night, November 4, 1928, the gambler took Inez Norton, his intimate for some years, to dinner at the Colony. While she continued on to the Rialto Theater, he stopped at Lindy's, then his favorite stamping ground. The preliminaries at this restaurant are clear: about 10:15

Beatrice Jackson at the Park Central Hotel switchboard received a request from Room 349, where a George Richards had registered, for a connection with Lindy's. The cashier, Abe Scher, heard a voice he didn't recognize:

"Tell Arnold Rothstein I want to talk to him."

He summoned Rothstein, who after a brief conversation walked out with Jimmy Meehan, saying:

"McManus wants to see me. I'm going to his room. I'll be back in half an hour."

He asked Meehan to hold his loaded automatic till his return.

He didn't live to reclaim it. The next person to see him, the next one who would confess to it, was the elevator operator at the servants' entrance, on 56th Street, of the Park Central: Vincent J. Kelly discovered him desperately clutching the banister. Rothstein said:

"I was shot. Get me an ambulance."

Kelly called a house detective, who called a cop. A City Hospital doctor attended the wounded man and he was removed to Polyclinic Hospital.

In the 12 hours remaining to him, he talked to a string of visitors, and wrote a will, but only one officer of the law bothered to question him, and for hardly a minute at that. Police didn't want to know any more; their trouble was, they knew too much. In Room 349 at the Park Central they seized an overcoat with the name George McManus embroidered in the lining. A comparison with a photo seemed to show he was the Richards registered there, and a maid so identified him.

McManus, or Richards, in a booth at 57th Street and Eighth Avenue, phoned his cronies for help. A car driven by an aide of Dutch Schultz picked him up and sped him to

142

a hideaway in a Bronx apartment. That was too far off, evidently, for the cops to find him, and he stayed there snugly for 24 days. Then he surrendered voluntarily, was tried and acquitted. The benignant law even gave him back his overcoat.

Rothstein's biographer Leo Katcher explained the failure to solve the murder:

"Too many politicians, too many gangsters, too much money, too many reputations joined in covering up the facts."

As heirs to Rothstein and the sovereignty of the Times Square underworld, Katcher listed a notorious crew: Lucky Luciano, Dutch Schultz, Frank Costello, Lepke Buchalter, Joe Adonis, Abe Reles, and Albert Anastasia. Anastasia was shot, Reles was a suicide or "liquidated." Together these men stood for Tammany misrule, for overlordship of garment industry gangsters, for international dope control, for Mafia and for Murder, Inc.

XI "I don't know
how it could
get much worse"

There was a church for Times Square before Times Square itself existed.

Holy Cross Roman Catholic Church, on the north side of 42nd just west of Eighth Avenue, was founded in 1852. In our century Father Francis P. Duffy was pastor till his death in 1932. Doughty chaplain of the "Fighting Irish," the 69th Regiment of New York, or the 165th Infantry, he carried on the tradition of several distinguished prelates. His successor, the Right Reverend Monsignor Joseph A. McCaffrey, came up from the sidewalks of New York, played football for Fordham and ran on its track team, and won the Silver Star and the Croix de Guerre at the front in World War I. Since 1924 he has served the New York City Police Department as chaplain, and he followed Father Duffy in the same office with the "Fighting Irish."

The northern end of Times Square, the thin narrow triangle from 45th Street to 47th, is properly Duffy Square in memory of Father Duffy. His honestly conventional statue, erected there thanks to the efforts of Father McCaffrey and his priests, refrains charitably from passing judgment on this unhallowed place. At the unveiling on a

Sunday in May 1937, surpliced altar boys elevated crucifix and candles in the presence of 30,000. With traffic halted an hour, the 69th marched past to the tune of "Onward Christian Soldiers." The bronze figure, by Charles Keck, is braced against a granite Celtic cross, the only cross in Times Square, which furthermore does not contain a single spire.

The presence of Father Duffy has never yet curbed the revelry around him, and it is even less likely to now that he must share the honors with George M. Cohan. This master of song and dance, also in a life-size bronze, has been mounted rudely right in front of the churchman, and back to him. But the unveiling of Cohan, on a September 1959 weekday, required a different kind of ceremony. Oscar Hammerstein II presided, and about 10,000 attended, including police, stage and screen personalities, and habitués of the crossroads. George Jessel, swinging a cane and a hat —the sculpture by George Lober has a cane and hat, too— was emcee. The singing was secular: "Give My Regards to Broadway."

The blatant worldliness of this section of the parish offends Father McCaffrey, who has written out of his warm heart:

"Adjacent to America's amusement center on 42nd Street stands a Roman Catholic church older than Times Square itself. More than a century ago, it was a parish of farmlands, uncultivated property, dirt roads, and horse-cars. Its spires towered above everything around it, but now they are dwarfed by the surrounding skyscrapers. In contrast to the pleasure and amusements and hurly-burly of the rest of Times Square, it is an oasis of peace and quiet and prayer."

The crossroads worships and prays by the old-time religion, revivalist, and tub-thumping. That's just what Times Square's old-time ways of sinning call for, and it's as obvious as the advertising and the merrymaking. The man who confesses his Lord on a sandwich board is typical:

"Look to Jesus and be saved!"

Or on one side of another placard nailed to a long stick you read, "The wicked shall be turned into Hell, and repent Psalm 9–17." If you look back after you pass, the other side presumably identifies the solemn, grubbing fellow carrying it: "This poor man cried and Jesus saved him." Accompanying each quotation, a painting depicts a kneeling figure described as "Way of Life" and a misshapen black blot supposedly symbolical of "Way of Death."

Evangelists stage a street-corner rally almost every night, with the American flag lashed to a hydrant and the speaker shaking a Bible in the often skeptical faces of the crowd he invariably attracts. The Salvation Army and the Episcopal church meet outdoors several times a week for sermon, prayer, and music. The Seventh-Day Adventists and Catholics backstop their determined confreres with regular church, Sunday school, and educational programs.

The Lord's most loyal and uncompromising emissary is Rose Harvel, small, bespectacled and wiry, who comes night after night to her chosen spot on 45th Street opposite the north side of the Hotel Astor.

She does not believe in turning away wrath with a soft answer, probably because she has suffered some relentless heckling. She hits back at Doubting Thomases as sharply as ever they nag at her. Besides the sarcastic and hostile listeners and the ones who argue just because they too want roles in the street scene, she draws a dependable circle of faithful, some of them attracted regularly by her earnest, shrill harangues.

"She's all right, that one," an old, bedraggled toothless admirer volunteers with an emphatic wag of her head.

A young man handing out Catholic leaflets near her followers defends her:

"We're for her. There's no conflict of creeds here. She's a Quaker, but she does the work of the Lord."

He paused while she disposed of a heckler, a taut jittery Negro girl who kept needling her. Arm in arm with a youth who seemed embarrassed by her vehemence, she grew almost hysterical, until the evangelist slapped her down in a piercing, unpleasant tone of voice, almost a fishwife's snarl, then turned abruptly to address another segment of her audience, leaving the Negro woman cross-examining the empty air.

The Catholic remarked: "We really like to have questions asked. It stirs up a crowd. But not dumb questions."

"Do you speak for the Quakers?" you ask her, and she snaps back: "I speak for Jesus!"

"Hey, Rosie!" some one else interrupts, but she goes on, about one hundred feet in from Broadway, extolling the Narrow Way.

Other speakers create a more relaxed mood with other audiences. A man attacking Catholicism, in this Square hemmed in by it, boasted "God gave me a head!" and a heckler got a laugh by retorting "Then use it!" But when another bystander challenged "How can woman's lovely skin come from an ape?" the soapbox orator earned his laugh by quickly asking his interlocutor: "What's wrong

with an ape? Are you trying to run down one of God's creatures?"

In Timesquare, as it has been spelt, you can hear a hymn sung if you happen by at the right hour of the right day in the right month of the right year. There used to be a tree at Christmas. The Easter breakfast served in the Hotel Astor to 5000 officers of the Police Department's Holy Name Society must spread some rich Christian aura even beyond the revolving doors. But it is too worldly a place for a church to prosper. The best it can do with a holy day is to recast it boisterously as a holiday, and it has never really accommodated its ways to religion.

Various denominations hopefully dispatch hard working missionaries, among the hardest working men and women in New York, and they never slacken in their devout labors. The nearest church, and the most influential as well as the oldest, is Holy Cross with its Father McCaffrey, doyen of the faithful of the entire area. Often he acts as spokesman for churches in general, as at the dedication in 1958 of the Times Square Public Information Center.

In a West 51st Street house where the animal trainers from the Madison Square Garden circus bunked three deep, so that the animal smell remained long after the odor of sanctity should have banished it, St. Paul's House has been established, Episcopal in support but interdenominational in practice. It operates under the leadership of a former Philadelphian, Creighton Dunlap, who served his apprenticeship under Rev. J. J. D. Hall, known as "Daddy" Hall, the "Bishop of Wall Street." Once a businessman, converted at an outdoor meeting himself, Dunlap believes unreservedly in outdoor meetings in New York, and he attracts a lot of attention at them if only because he stands a lanky six feet six and a half inches. The Army drafted him, and as good as had him in its ranks when the recruiting officer asked how tall he was. It amounted to an inch too much, which dropped him from 1-A to 4-F, he recalls:

"I could have fired a rifle as well as anyone, I think. But at least I got into the army of the Lord, where height is no handicap."

Saturdays and Sundays he addresses pick-up crowds at 42nd Street and Eighth Avenue. A lot of people attend regularly. Once in a while some one yells from the window of a passing auto "Drop Dead!" or "Go to Aitch!" as he expresses it. He proudly remembers many whom his mission house has succored: a youth who arrived in the city all set for a binge but changed his mind on hearing a message from Dunlap "that gripped his heart"; one teacher confused about his belief who "found faith at St. Paul's" and another who "accepted Christ and came to grips with the Lord at our meetings"; an alcoholic who reformed; an actor who had forgotten God and was saved; a newsboy who, surmounting the baleful influence of his neighborhood associates, came to Sunday school and to everyone's amusement as well as satisfaction announced "I'm safe!" and a Negro couple from New Jersey:

"I just felt we ought to go to Times Square," the woman said humbly. "I thought there was nothing left for us who had lost our boy but go to Times Square"—where they were solaced by Dunlap's assurance that a child in his innocence would ascend straight to heaven, and all the straighter since his death had driven his parents to worship and prayer.

"It's an area of many broken homes, and perverts, pimps, slit-knife boys and gangs," Dunlap acknowledged with regret. "But on the whole the denizen here and the visitor are good people. There may be dumb ones but I can show you bright ones; there may be sordid but there are fine, too."

People who live and work in Times Square like Times Square people. "Bright," "good," and "fine" is not all they say of the folks next door. "The people in Times Square have more time than other folks here, so they're more courteous," the Adventists' New York Center reports. Father McCaffrey, whose parish extends from Broadway and Seventh Avenue to Tenth Avenue, praises the coming generation enthusiastically: "There are some of the neatest, politest children you ever saw right here." "The best people as well as the worst go through Times Square," says Captain James Leland Bozman of the Salvation Army Corps which has been on duty there almost 75 years. Bozman continues:

"The Times Square crowd is in need of church. There are as many people in New York with a spiritual lack as you'll find elsewhere, and though Africa may be a rich field for missionary work, what's wrong with carrying it on right here? So many stop in and gladly sit in a Christian atmosphere like ours, often a whole family comes together, there are as many men as women, but not so many children for this is no place for them.

"There are a great many low-income people in this area. In scores of places people occupy one room with bed and dresser and chair and that's where they sleep, but not where they live, they don't live anywhere, really, they just wander the streets. Show business has-beens hang around, or live here out of nostalgia, and also a lot of people in show business at this minute have rooms right in Times Square."

The New York Center described it in the same terms: "It's a neighborhood of unattached people, living alone."

The Salvation Army post on West 49th near Seventh Avenue is one door from a café with a nearly nude floor show and two from a movie house which features Brigitte Bardot among other temporal distractions. The new quarters have a recessed glass front sheltering passers-by from the weather and allowing them, thanks to a loud-speaker, to hear a sermon; often some one comes inside to join the service. Folks in the sticks save their money, they visit the big city, they've heard of this area and gravitate toward it, and they promptly lose their money and their shirt to stores doing a hustling one-shot business, selling a customer once and hoping never to lay eyes on him again, Bozman charged. He found fault with the display advertisements:

"There's a great deal of deception behind those false fronts. Lots of people are taken in along there. Then they come around to the Salvation Army."

He explained: "This is the closest spot to the spot where they went broke."

"We have Old Folks Night, Ladies' Home League, and Men's Fellowship League. It's just like home for a lot of our visitors."

"The crossroads looks garish," the Army captain continued, "but it is really sad. Lots of people want to escape from the small town, so they bring their problems here. They are unhappy, so they seek adventure. A man might earn and save and strike out for something new, he has a yearning to travel, he gets to New York City and sooner or later to Times Square. Other towns are not so hard to buck, this is tough, so the man at the end of a long string of hard luck, and at the end of his rope, too, is apt to wind up at the Times Square station of the Salvation Army. Maybe more social misfits appear here because Times Square is really the place where the misfit fits."

Bozman holds assemblies four times a week at 49th Street and Seventh Avenue, with a stand for the uniformed speakers, a pair of flags, music and amplification.

Like Dunlap, he felt Billy Graham had done nobly by the Lord in his campaign in the city at large and in particular his climactic rally in Times Square in September 1957. Almost two million people had seen and heard the evangelist since the middle of May, and he expected 50,000—a modest number for this crossroads. Dunlap believed Graham should have been allowed to speak in the Square itself; instead, police had him park his trailer-truck platform astride Broadway just below 42nd Street, with his congregation to the south. The crowd, unusually hushed for midtown, stretched down to 37th Street and to the north for some distance beyond 43rd. The single block from 42nd to 43rd was closed to the public.

Four hundred people gathered at one barrier by four o'clock that Sunday afternoon, and 6000 by five for a program scheduled to start at seven. Police figured the attendance at 75,000, but Graham emphatically disputed this, claiming he had never addressed so large a group and estimating it at 200,000. Graham's backers, in contrast to the street-corner orators, had no kind word for the police, though if New York's "finest" seemed unfriendly to the Protestant revivalist, they performed their normal duties with perfunctory thoroughness: 500 officers reported no auto accident, passed out no tickets to drivers, found eight persons mostly middle-aged needing medical aid, rescued three lost children, and arrested two pickpockets.

The *Times* announced the meeting in the course of it on the traveling news line so that the evangelist could look over his shoulder and read his name in electric lights. Despite the inevitable voluble cynics hanging around the fringes of the phenomenal concourse, many of the devout listened with tears in their eyes. Four films billed on nearby marquees suggested topics to Graham: *The Ten Commandments, The Lonely Man, The Walking Dead,* and *Love in the Afternoon.* He defined the Square as a center of amusement, moneymaking, merrymaking, and drinking, and said:

"Tonight for a few moments it is being turned into a great cathedral as a symbol of the spiritual revival that is now in progress in America."

Father McCaffrey yearns for a lasting spiritual revival in the Square itself. Does the place affect his flock?

"Nobody on Tenth Avenue ever sets foot in Times Square," he answered. "They have their own neighborhood movies."

In his opinion the crossroads has deteriorated steadily in the twenty-five years since he began his ministry at Holy Cross. "I'm getting a parish of parking lots."

Calling to mind the good theater of long ago, he mentioned *Abie's Irish Rose* and praised the Republic, New Amsterdam, Apollo, Lyric, and Harris all for offering worth-while legitimate stage fare—in the past.

But as he glanced back along 42nd Street from the sanctuary of his rectory, his severe eye encountered much to condemn. You could buy anything on Sunday along there, he lamented. Any store was allowed to stay open as long as it sold souvenirs such as the Statue of Liberty in a tiny casting, and imitation bronze Empire State Buildings, and religious pictures and statuettes, too. You found them right off on the counters near the entrance, but keep on going and in back there were spread out shamelessly books of photos of nudes, or big colored enlargements of them.

You were apt to be cheated, too, he claimed. CLOSING TONIGHT, the sign in the window advertised. Didn't they close every night? Yet they tricked you into expecting bargain prices. You preferred charges to the police, they advised an appeal to the small-claims court, and who would sacrifice a couple of entire days trying to recover $3 or $4? Who especially would if he came from out of town and must leave? And who above all would depend on that so much as a shyster salesman or a phony auctioneer? The city recently summonsed half-a-dozen auctioneers, accused them of hiring shills to raise bids falsely, and either deprived them of their licenses or enjoined them from practicing any more in Times Square. But the police were not helping so much in other matters, he complained. Raids on a bookstore resulted in fourteen arrests for hawking pornography, but not a person spent a day in jail for it, the priest charged. In one movie house alone the authorities picked up fourteen degenerates in a single month. As for the films themselves, you only had to read the signs.

"They cut out live burlesque," Father McCaffrey remembered gratefully. "Whatever you think of Mayor La Guardia, he had nerve. But these second-run pictures are worse: nudist camps, what young boys and girls should never know, sex in school.

"People come here, everybody comes here," he continued resentfully, "for it is the most advertised place in the city, or in the world. They look at Fifth Avenue and see the most money in the world, they come to Times Square and see the toughest part. This is the toughest part of New York. It is worse than Coney Island ever was."

Can Times Square get better? "I don't know how it could get much worse!"

XII "Hell's Kitchen isn't even a frying pan any more"

The Police Department, its blue uniforms the commonest sign of the hand of government in Times Square, does not agree with Father McCaffrey's severe verdict; it is more charitable. A check of the docket proves that this place, however sinful its past, has reformed. New York has plenty of hotter spots. Out of 81 precincts in all, this one would not fall in the top quarter of the list for major crime.

Precinct No. 16, it stretches from Fifth Avenue to the Hudson, and from 42nd Street to 50th. It contains big department stores, hotels, theaters, tenements and apartments with a permanent population of 45,000, and the waterfront and piers for some ocean liners. Patrolmen like assignment to this "premium" post, with something always doing and a limitless diversity. Over 200 of them work out of the 47th Street station house, a barracks of a headquarters almost a hundred years old. It antedates Times Square. It antedates Hell's Kitchen, which was that overcrowded region west to the river and southward, the festering slums that produced the criminals that ran the dives that produced the criminals and so on viciously.

Now the guardians of the law joke, "Hell's Kitchen isn't even a frying pan any more."

The ghosts of Rosenthal and Rothstein are laid. Instead of gunning for desperadoes, the officers, surprisingly, blame their worst headaches on the totally unarmed men who hawk roasted chestnuts out of dilapidated baby carriages; the "fags" along 42nd Street; the more intemperate evangelists; and the beggars. They continue:

"There is only one legitimate night club left, the Latin Quarter. There isn't a single house of prostitution. The sale of dope has been cut way down—only four arrests for it were made in the first ten months of 1959."

Since the Square is largely a rendezvous for transients, dope isn't commercially feasible. The "push," as they name the seller, must be acquainted with his customers—the law catches up with him most often by "putting a tail" on known users; he doesn't dare do business with the unfamiliar throngs at this crossroads. Prostitution is well under control, too. A few girls hang around late at night—girls maybe from poverty-stricken mining towns, their squalid histories show, or, if they are Negroes, from the South. If they didn't earn a pile of money in the war when countless soldiers and sailors had pay checks to squander, they have had little chance since.

The decrease in these offenses can be explained simply: money is scarcer today, or tonight, in Times Square, though it is more bustling than ever. It has lost the big spenders to exclusive clubs or expensive restaurants and bars farther east. It attracts principally the man with a couple of bucks, who eats in a hurry for less than a dollar, or gets his excitement out of "Fascination," a game of skill, technically, by the accepted definition, though some peo-

ple "live for it the way they do for bingo," officers claim. What they mean is, that the lack of money is the root of some good, too.

Even the "fags" operate within rigid economic levels. The rich ones don't prey on passers-by here, where the costumes are dungarees, or shirts with open collar. The boys who loiter mostly along 42nd Street rate as law enforcement's problem No. 2. Plain-clothesmen nab some, but they are not easy to identify. They don't bear the marks of effeminacy usually attributed to their kind, and do not solicit boldly like streetwalkers. The arrests are often repeats, half from out of town. If these characters are subjected to a specially vigilant check, it is not because they commit overt illegal acts here, but because, despite their seeming soft ways, their habits often involve them in violence. A fairy in a bar accosts a man too drunk to know what he's doing; but sobered up, simply not the right breed, he swings on the fellow who propositioned him. There is also the unwary homo tricked by a blackmailer, and that can result in a fight.

"Bottle babies," or drunks, congregate south of 42nd Street, in the next man's precinct. Many of them were born or brought up in Times Square, and sentiment draws them back. A clerk presiding over the station-house blotter comments:

"Funny, too. I don't know why, but quite a few others come from Boston."

"But our worst problem," police readily admit, "is peddlers.

"In the spring they sell orchids. In the summer, ice cream. Fall and winter we have the vendor of roasted chestnuts always with us. Now understand, we don't object to the public eating chestnuts, or a man earning his living by selling them, or selling orchids. But if there wasn't any restriction at all on peddlers in this Square, they would fill it wall to wall and not even leave room enough for a buyer, or just a plain visitor. So we control it. We don't let anyone sell here—and even so there isn't always room for the rest of you.

"The chestnut man cuts out the insides of an old baby carriage and fits in a pan of coals and a stock of his goods, and then wheels the contraption onto a Times Square walk. If he is lucky, if he chooses a good corner and no police-man scares him away, you know what he earns in a night? Twenty-five dollars, or thirty-five, and with a real break, fifty. So we arrest him, the judge fines him one or two bucks for obstructing the walk, that's nothing to him, it's like forking over a license fee, he's right back the next night."

Juvenile delinquents—though the phrase is too general—do not flock here. For one reason, not many young people live in the neighborhood. Those who do gather, even when they attract unwelcome attention, are not always delin-quents:

"Young fellows come down in a body from a university, they wear costumes and masks, it's a fraternity initiation, fifty of them snake-dance around, it slows down traffic, drivers blow their horns till it's pandemonium, somebody gets elbowed and objects to it, there's a complaint. So what? This is not the juvenile delinquency the papers write about, even though the youths are juveniles and there is a technical delinquency.

"Then Negro boys from Harlem shine shoes. They set up their boxes by the foot of the building walls, along comes a pedestrian, he's looking at the waterfall, or the news sign, or anyway head in the air. So he trips, and the city gets taken proper for damages. So we call the boy in, and then his parents, we explain what it's all about, maybe we make out a card for the kid but it's not an arrest, and it's not juvenile delinquency. It isn't even this precinct's juvenile delinquency when a gang from outside invades and kills two perfectly good juveniles, as happened two months back."

But the attitude, understandably forgiving toward these youngsters, turns a little sour and perhaps defensive when it comes to the evangelists and their audiences. New York police once made a test case of an arrest for speaking outdoors without a permit—unless the culprit made a test case of New York police. His conviction was appealed, and sustained repeatedly right up to the Supreme Court, which reversed it on the grounds of interference with freedom of worship and speech.

Corner spielers consequently are allowed both freedoms completely: they are free to talk, and free to talk about religion. But time and place are subject to the strictest control based on practical considerations like obstructing the walks and the flow of traffic. The evangelist must display an American flag. He is banned from Broadway and relegated to a side street, and must stop whenever his crowd gets in the public's way—or whenever the officer on duty thinks it does.

He can be arrested for disorderly conduct, and so can obnoxious listeners. This is not uncommon, apparently, for tempers flare and words lead to blows, or The Word does more often than by its nature it should. Most of the speakers are accused of being a sort of maverick. They don't expound the staple religions, but crackpot ideas, and in fact attack Protestants, Catholics, and Jews. Such criticism is quite legal until some citizen registers a specific complaint.

"None of the regular big three religions has ever asked for a corner for its own use," the police say in behalf of their touchy attitude.

The beggars, finally, operate in outright defiance of the law, and get away with it handsomely.

"The Times Square crowds take the side of the beggar, and particularly the blind man," an officer pointed out. "We go up to a blind fellow practically with our cap in our hand, we tell him to feel our badge so he knows we're really a policeman. Then we try to argue him out of soliciting.

"A lot of the blind live in a 49th Street hotel that caters to them, and to their wives, too, who sometimes also beg. You see, not a one is on relief, we investigated and found out. They earn their own livings. They're businessmen, can you believe it! The police should interfere with businessmen? This is the American spirit. They're in the best-known spot in the country, and they're on their own. This is free enterprise."

Epilogue

Times Square, impervious to criticism, might even like it, however, if it were strung up in lights. Elmer Rice decided he hated Broadway. One writer complained that celebrations in the night spots "put to blush the wildest capers of the Moulin Rouge, Maxim's and other notorious places in Paris"; and a second also borrowed a French term of condemnation, as though America didn't provide a comparison wicked enough: he branded it the *parc aux cerfs*, the deer park, for the debauchery of kings.

Let's take a last look around, we shall always return but this is a tourist's eye *au revoir:* one more glimpse of the crossroads where Minsky battled for burlesque against the adamant license commissioner; one more glimpse of Hotalings newsstand where out of towners grow chummy and dream of home sweet home; of the Paramount where a mad bomber planted a homemade bomb, and hundreds mad in their own different fashion massed for a hysterical welcome to Frank Sinatra and again to rock 'n' roller Alan Freed; of jazz dives in the basement or at street level where hangers-on go tzg-tzg-tzg and snap their fingers and fling back their heads; and of the overflowing walks where the legless cripple propels himself on a dolly, the Seeing Eye dog earns his keep as well as his master's, the evangelists give out their pitch.

We come in along 42nd Street from the Port Authority Bus Terminal, which accommodates more passengers than Grand Central. Except perhaps for the Apollo which programs foreign films, it is an "awful street," according to a producer whom it ruined; it is the worst approach. The fanged monster leers, the shell explodes and bodies hurtle through the air, the sneering villain will rape the terrified girl, the man leaps for his foe with drawn knife, the boy buries his head between the bawd's breasts—all on movie posters. Fellows slouch against the mudguards of parked cars. There is an ambulant cast, moving east moving west moving in idle circles, like figures from limbo. The faces are not pitiful and tragic like Kaethe Kollwitz's, not laughable and congenial like Daumier's, but wretched, empty, half-human, antipathetic like the vapid coarse creations of Paul Cadmus.

The drunk with a slobbered chin, as ravenous for an audience as the actor in the legitimate theater, does a staggering befuddled dance. He winds a rubbery arm around a passer-by and gets an angry shove in response; his bottle of gin or rotgut slips from limp fingers. If we escape the sot, we are trapped by the ubiquitous bore, also determined to impress us, who like many denizens of Times Square proper just around the corner has an act to perform, a public gesture of which he must deliver himself. He asks a direction, and then explains, "I got a date with a good egg and I don't want to break it" and rolling his eyes he walks off to accost a score of other strangers before he exhausts his exhibitionist vein and gets the guffaws as

necessary to him as drink or dope to another man. He is part ham—he is part Hammerstein, part Rector, part Ochs, part Paul Potter, part Rosenthal and Rothstein, part gawker and gawked-at. He is a show-off, he can't endure being ignored. Times Square is his stage. This is the crossroads catharsis.

Or we come up into the Square itself by subway, a short climb at 43rd Street where the BMT ceiling is less than three feet below the pavement. Twenty years ago a guidebook said 200,000 people welled up there daily from underground. The New York City Transit Authority, claiming the traffic peak occurred in 1947, now counts 135,000 passengers buying tokens every 24 hours to leave the place. It's impossible to estimate the number traveling by the buses that roll in undependable irregular batches north on Sixth and Eighth Avenues and south on Seventh and Broadway.

Even with a dozen more visits to this bewildering area, you can't straighten out the snarl of streets. Starting at Central Park, Broadway buses run down Seventh Avenue, and Seventh Avenue buses down Broadway till they reach Times Square where they veer in the announced directions. Because Seventh Avenue changes to Broadway for two blocks below 44th, Broadway touches 42nd twice yet intersects it only once. The Astor Hotel is on Seventh, the Paramount right beside it on Broadway; the Times Tower is impossibly situated between Broadway and Broadway.

Or you come in along a darker side street. You pass a hotel entrance bare and uninviting; a garage with gas pumps, and signs: Exit, No Exit, Entrance, Blow Your Horn, Slow; a lunchroom; a liquor store; a barroom lighted cozily giving out music and laughter. What vice there is, instead of flaunting itself right in the Square, operates sneakily in these dim antechambers east and west. Out of one door a woman rushes to hail a cab. It pulls up, she leans in the lowered window to dicker at length. She retreats to the walk while the driver works in closer to the curb. Four men emerge from a dingy hotel at a quick pace, supporting a woman between them, feet first and lying out flat as on a stretcher. They take short steps. The edge of her light skirt blows up above the tops of rolled stockings. One man orders, "Cover up her face," and another does so with her scarf. It is the face of a white woman. The men, all smiling fixedly, are Orientals; they have an apologetic air, they seem velly solly—our dear sister—taken ill—so sad. They lift her into the cab and climb in themselves, it moves away, the other woman disappears unconcernedly. Is it too much drink, a fainting spell, a sleeping powder? Is it nothing at all, or a hair-raising chapter for Thomas Burke's *Limehouse Nights* or for *The Mysteries of New York* to match Eugene Sue's *Mysteries of Paris?*

In the Square itself anything can happen and anything does. A young man in a silk hat and a pretty girl in a wedding gown and veil mount to the floor of a big truck and are married. Their guests are the unknown public with smiles, stares, shrugs, and inquisitive glances. The bridegroom is jobless, the ceremony is free, they get $5000 worth of gifts and the point of it is, that the movie *Guys and Dolls* will be premièred in an hour. Or you catch unbelievingly the smell of horses. The check reins off and heads drooping, a team is halted by the curb, harnessed to a black hearse with festoons of white satin and the solemn adornment of gold tassels, all for another movie, *Count Dracula*. It's a show for the sake of a show. There is even another horse: Paul Revere difmounts and hitches it to a poft in front of the Sheraton-Aftor; he has ridden from Bofton on his way to Philadelphia to advertise a hoftelry opening there. A San Francisco cable car, 1907 vintage, on rubber tires and manned by a uniformed crew, drives around to promote a TV program.

Sometimes it's just fun, nobody gets paid, nobody sells anything. A college boy for a fraternity initiation equips himself with a five-foot bow and steel-tipped arrows, and invites passers-by to let him shoot an apple off their heads— when in fact the police picked him up for disorderly conduct, the prosecutor heedlessly asked why he mistook Times Square for Sherwood Forest, and he might have asked in turn why the prosecutor mistook William Tell for Robin Hood. The charge was dismissed. A second youth with only a fishing pole for weapon tramps past in a farmer's sloppy straw hat, a raincoat and rubber boots— there is a moon overhead. Among his companions, unshaven, in dungarees, looking as though they all hiked up from the old fishing hole, one carries a three-foot fish made of rubber.

Even worn seriously, the styles are as varied: the white top of a sailor, the black gown of a priest, a checkered green cap, the visors of soldiers, guides, and chauffeurs, missionaries in black robes, hats and beards, the pearl-gray, broad-brimmed sombrero, the tam-o'-shanter, the scarf, the hat with a theater stub or gay feather tucked in the ribbon, and headgear in every material, shape, size, and color that comes, with the purchaser's name, from Maxie's Hats, which specializes in the ludicrous.

This spot is guaranteed to draw a crowd. The narrow entrance right on the street is half-filled by a man who whistles deafeningly while he makes a sewing machine hum. The shelves are stacked with wares red orange yellow green blue violet, the light is bright, the radio blares. A sight-seer and his companion break into a dance on the walk, and kick high front and back, the onlookers clap in unison for them, a girl kisses her sailor smack on the mouth, an aged couple gapes slack-jawed and suspects it is Sodom.

People watch the flame lick up around steaks on charcoal broilers. But the more popular eating spot serves pizza pies. The deft white-capped cook in Childs window tossed flapjacks for decades to fascinate the hungry. Now they assemble for the pizza pie *artiste*. Nonchalant, he is an accomplished actor. He reaches for a gob of prepared dough, thumps it on the bread board, flattens it, kneads it, works over it like a sculptor with clay. When it's a foot across, he levitates it on his fingertips, flings it spinning overhead, twirls it like a cowboy playing with a looped lasso, my, the audiences gasp, lookit, they exclaim, he flops it back on the board, smooths it, dusts it, and starts dishing out the relish and other spicy fillings—pizza pie, sneers a filthy old hag who wants to steal the show from him, that's not how to say what he makes, leave these dirty foreigners hannul our food, huh! and she stomps off cursing.

Crowds also gather before the giant at the Odditorium, the winking Mr. Peanut with his cane, the noise that explodes from the Metropole bar, the jazz mart on the fringes of the Square. Or they eye askance the tricks and toys in the Playlands, like the joker eight-column dummy newspaper headline *JACK HAMILTON IN TOWN, CALL GIRLS EXHAUSTED*—they supply any name they wish and mail it to their friends.

But there are things you won't blush to tell the folks about, for instance two plaques. One on the Times Tower identifies the paper which gave the Square its name. The other cater-cornered across Broadway at 43rd says the only dramatist born in the Square dramatists made famous is Eugene O'Neill, whose birthplace was the former Barrett House on that site. Just a few steps east you could see, if bulky air-conditioning machinery and dust didn't foil you, the costly gilt which adorned the gaming room at the old Metropole restaurant where Rosenthal was slain. Back farther north, looking down across the place forlornly amid the racket, dazzle, and towering signs, stand the statues of Father Duffy and George M. Cohan.

More Cohan than Duffy has survived. Not far from the reverend chaplain was Minsky's Gaiety. The ban on all girlie shows was announced 24 hours before the priest's bronze likeness was unveiled; and the stubborn Minsky got an injunction against the cops though it was good only through that first, and last, day. The papers said the poor strip-teaser innocents left their jobs weeping, and their union painted an even more pathetic and respectable picture: they were all hard working and decent, and actual figures proved three out of four furnished the main support of their families or relatives.

Mayor La Guardia hailed "the beginning of the end of incorporated filth"; Patrick Cardinal Hayes declared, "I have seldom received news that brings more joy to my heart." That last night, a Friday, the Gaiety was advertising "gorgeous glorified maids and models in a landslide of loveliness." It was Christopher Morley who hit on the pat name for burlesque houses: "rump Parliaments." Police now speak of "Queens County," and some women, black as well as white, for there is no segregation in this business, stir up trade on the east side of the Square.

But overlaying this garish and wanton core is a thick coating of sentiment, as at Hotalings newsstand. Men and women who never met back in Birmingham or Walla Walla, and wouldn't have spoken if they had, encounter each other buying the home-town papers, their eyes light up, they shake, they walk off arm in arm, well, a small world after all, imagine! A woman who has not heard from the daughter she quarreled with is overjoyed by a message of reconciliation in a Texas personals column. Even the FBI and New York police recognize this sentimental presence, and watch for elopers. Of course newlyweds hunt there for their names on the society page. But sentiment can cause trouble. The FBI, parked by the curb, ambushed an embezzler who couldn't endure not knowing how everything was going back in Meriden, Connecticut.

Maybe it is mainly the visitors who are sentimental. They have ready silver for panhandlers with cup or banjo. Some sharpers do the restaurants out of a meal, some honest drudges laboriously fish coins up through the sidewalk gratings. But the plain outright beggar is always there. A man in the tow of a harnessed dog taps his white cane to steer an insecure path along Seventh Avenue. He walks so slowly that one block uses up half an hour. He stops once to light a cigarette. Passers-by—the Chicagoan, Bostonian, clerk, machinist, nurse, switchboard operator, electrician, carpenter—lean over to pat the German police dog, who submits indifferently. He pokes his nose into a woman's bag, but exasperatingly and embarrassingly he spurns a spatula of hamburg dropped on the walk before him by the tender-hearted lunchroom clerk—who regularly sells his customers exactly the same meat. Yet the dog serves his master well, since in that short patrol he collects donations from three women and eight men—the usual proportion.

The public spreads out a paper and sits on the stone border around Father Duffy, rests an elbow on the Elpine counter to drink orangeade, fingers magazines in the rack, buys candy at Barton's and ice cream at Howard Johnson's, and fancy hats at Maxie's.

Then the buyer throws away the container. This is the city's heaviest "pedestrian litter" section, in the Sanitation Department's phrase. Cigarette butts, packages, ticket stubs, paper bags, newspapers, sandwich wrappings— about six tons a day are collected by two trucks and six men from the 200 trash baskets between 42nd Street and 50th. And the crossroads population misses the baskets with 1200 pounds more every 24 hours.

But people have other things on their minds. The girl mincing past says:

"We're lookin' aroun' like we're tourists see an' he says . . ."

The woman: "Let's go somewheres, anywheres I can get off my feet!"

The man jeers: "Big operator, big operator my eye, ha!"

The gossip maintains: "She shoulden ever of married him!"

The blind beggar holds out a piece of money and pleads in a fleshless, disembodied voice: "Somebody tell me what this is please tell me what this is please . . ."

A distraught woman walking along by herself singsongs incomprehensibly. It's a sort of keening. She waves a torn envelope and two or three loose dollar bills. Her face is

177

tired and vacant, her gray hair disheveled, tears shine in her eyes. Move on, says the cop. What's the matter? she demands. Move on, he orders. She bursts into sobs. He shrugs. She stumbles off. Boys on bicycles—red wheels, bumpers, rearview mirrors, horns and bells—scoot scarily almost under a racing truck, or behind a bus, and miss a pedestrian by an inch, and fly out of sight.

Through a hidden door lies the headquarters of ANTA, the American National Theater & Academy; and its chief, Robert W. Dowling, a theater owner, too, talks about Times Square's prospects:

"Lincoln Center will improve the tone of this place if only because it will attract more culturally minded people to the city. But I doubt any effect on the theater district from the new development at Broadway in the Sixties. The theaters are here, right here, to stay. They tried more than once to get above Central Park and never succeeded.

"The Square began to lose quality in World War I. When as a boy I went to dinner with my father at the Knicker-bocker, we might sit beside Caruso, who lived in that hotel. That sort of experience couldn't occur here now. The movies have hurt. But the movies, too, are learning. They are no longer so interested in the mass audience of any-body and everybody with a couple of bucks. The façades of both the Helen Hayes and the Lunt-Fontanne Theaters just around the corner have been beautified and floodlit. Loew's State is reducing from 3000 seats to 1200; we are cutting down our Astor to the same extent."

The Astor, opened in 1906, used to house Cohan's shows, and turned to movies first in 1914. The remodeled "luxury theater" contains two abstract paintings 45 feet high and

97 feet long, and a third 25 by 10 feet, or some 9000 square feet of canvas.

"We like to think of the new Astor as the Museum of Modern Art of Times Square where millions of tourists and moviegoers will have an opportunity to enjoy the best of contemporary abstract art," Dowling says, and continues:

"When the theaters were centered at 14th Street, and then 23rd, and 34th, they had no substantial real estate backing. They were all alone in neighborhoods of cheap flats and boardinghouses. In Times Square they have behind them invaluable land richly developed. The Times-Life-Sports Illustrated building has just gone up over on Sixth Avenue. A skyscraper is planned at Eighth Avenue and 42nd Street. That is, you see improvement both east and west. Even without that, Times Square won't change for the simple reason it can't help itself. It can't help being the hub of transportation. It is the easiest place to get to for the most number of people."

Despite Father McCaffrey's complaint about parking lots, they are better than the tumble-down improvements they replace, and new structures are bound to arrive on them sometime.

We find the last word in books. In the 1930s Frank Gray Griswold charged stuffily that at the end of last century, "A first-night audience consisted of all the best and most cultured people in the city, they were nearly all acquainted with one another. A first-night audience at the present time is a mob from Bohemia, and today a native New Yorker seldom meets an acquaintance at the play."

Less than ten years ago the more broad-minded Simeon Strunsky warned: "You must not take too seriously the let-

179

ters to the newspapers in which people bewail the degradation of Times Square."

A few years later Chiang Yee wrote: "For many ages yet there will be only one Times Square."

Bibliography

CARNIVAL CROSSROADS is an evocation and estimate of Times Square, not a guidebook. But the authors have filled its pages with a guidebook-like profusion of names, places and dates. Where sources were contradictory and explanation cumbersome, they made their own choices, and hope they were the happy ones. Here from among the 200 books in which they found scattered items of information are minimal lists:

The following five books deserve special mention:

Berger, Meyer: *The Story of the New York Times 1851–1951.* New York: Simon and Schuster, 1951.

Cowley, Malcolm, editor: *Writers at Work.* New York: Viking, 1958.

Frohman, Daniel: *Daniel Frohman Presents.* New York: Lee Furman, 1937.

Howells, William Dean: *Impressions and Experiences.* New York: Harper, 1896.

Irving, Washington: Diedrich Knickerbocker: *Wolfert Webber,* or *Golden Dreams.* From *A Book of the Hudson* edited by Geoffrey Crayon. New York: Putnam, 1849.

Other helpful works are:

Bliven, Bruce, Jr.: *Battle for Manhattan.* New York: Holt, 1955–56.

Blumenthal, George, and Arthur H. Menkin: *My Sixty Years in Show Business.* New York: Olympia, 1936.

Chiang Yee: *The Silent Traveller in New York.* London: Methuen, 1950.

Clarke, Donald Henderson: *In the Reign of Rothstein*. New York: Vanguard, 1929.

Davis, Elmer: *History of the New York Times*. 1851–1921. New York: New York Times, 1921.

De Valois, Ninette: *Come Dance with Me*. New York: World, 1958.

Griswold, Frank Gray: *After Thoughts*. New York: Harper, 1936.

Hawkins, Stuart: *New York, New York*. New York: Wilfred Funk, 1957.

Jenkins, Stephen: *The Greatest Street in the World*. New York: Putnam's, 1911.

Katcher, Leo: *The Big Bankroll*. New York: Harper, 1959.

Kirkland, Alexander: *Rector's Naughty '90s Cookbook*. New York: Doubleday, 1949.

Klein, Alexander, editor: *The Empire City*. New York: Rinehart, 1955.

Klein, Henry H.: *Sacrificed: The Story of Police Lieutenant Charles Becker*. New York: Printer: Isaac Goldman Co., 1927.

——, *My 40 Year Fight for Justice*. New York: Pamphlet, publisher not listed, 1953.

Kouwenhoven, John A.: *The Columbia Historical Portrait of New York*. New York: Doubleday, 1954.

Laurie, Joe, Jr.: *Vaudeville: From the Honky-tonks to the Palace*. New York: Holt, 1953.

Loesser, Frank, Jo Swerling and Abe Burrows: *Guys and Dolls*. From *The Modern Theatre*, editor, Eric Russell Bentley. New York: Doubleday, 1956.

Macdonald, Mary: *Amazing New York*. London: Andrew Melrose, 1913.

Mayer, Grace A.: *Once Upon a City*. New York: Macmillan, 1958.

Monahan, Michael: *New Adventures*. New York: George H. Doran, 1917.

Morris, Lloyd: *Incredible New York*. New York: Random House, 1951.

New York City. Editors of *Look* and Frederick Lewis Allen. Boston and New York: Houghton Mifflin, 1948.

New York City Guide and Almanac 1957-1958. New York University Press. New York: New York University Press, 1958.

Potter, Paul: *The Girl from Rector's*. Produced at Weber's Theater, New York, 1909.

Rector, George: *The Girl from Rector's*. New York: Doubleday, Page, 1927.

Still, Bayard: *Mirror for Gotham*. New York: New York University Press, 1956.

Stokes, I. N. Phelps: *The Iconography of Manhattan Island 1498-1909*. New York: Robert H. Dodd, 1915.

Strong, George Templeton: *The Diary of George Templeton Strong*. Edited by Allan Nevins and Milton Halsey Thomas. New York: Macmillan, 1952.

Strunsky, Simeon: *No Mean City*. New York: Dutton, 1944.

Zukor, Adolph: *Influence of the Motion Picture*. From *Broadway: The Grand Canyon of American Business*. New York: Broadway Association, 1926.

Assorted pamphlets, bulletins, American scenic and Historic Preservation Society reports and Proceedings of the Board of Aldermen; *Harper's Monthly*, *Munsey's*, and *Everybody's* magazines, and several newspapers yielded information bountifully. There is a special indebtedness to the New York *Times*, with its proprietary interest in the Square, for details of many events and for items of various sorts, for instance, the ride of Paul Revere and the confusion between William Tell and Robin Hood.

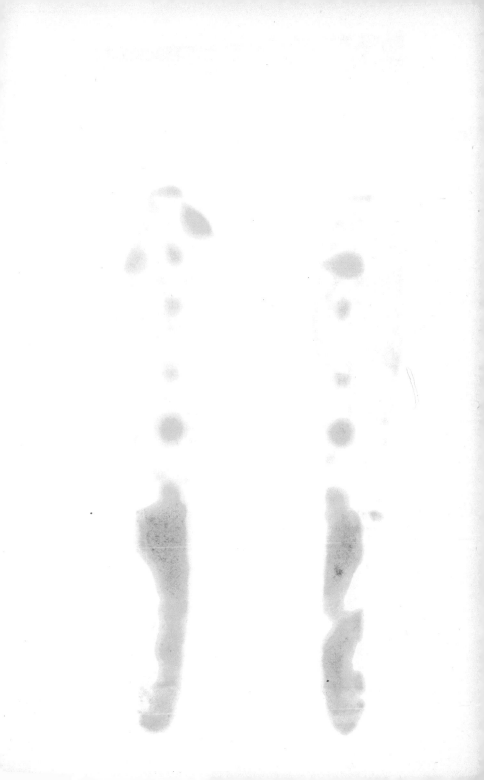

9/60

41755

ROGERS, WILLIAM
   CARNIVAL CROSSROADS.

DATE DUE	
MAR 12 2015	
APR 01 2015	